JAR THE FLOOR

BY CHERYL L. WEST

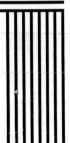

DRAMATISTS
PLAY SERVICE
INC.

JAR THE FLOOR
Copyright © 2002, Cheryl L. West

All Rights Reserved

SPECIAL NOTE

Anyone receiving permission to produce JAR THE FLOOR is required to give credit to the Author as sole and exclusive Author of the Play on the title page of all programs distributed in connection with performances of the Play and in all instances in which the title of the Play appears for purposes of advertising, publicizing or otherwise exploiting the Play and/or a production thereof. The name of the Author must appear on a separate line, in which no other name appears, immediately beneath the title and in size of type equal to 50% of the size of the largest, most prominent letter used for the title of the Play. No person, firm or entity may receive credit larger or more prominent than that accorded the Author. The following acknowledgment must appear on the title page in all programs distributed in connection with performances of the Play:

JAR THE FLOOR was originally produced by Parkland College
Champaign, Illinois, in 1989.

The professional premier was at the Empty Space Theatre
Seattle, Washington, in 1991.

The play was produced in New York by the Second Stage Theatre,
Carole Rothman, Artistic Director; Carol Fishman, Managing Director, in 1999.

SPECIAL NOTE ON SONGS AND RECORDINGS

For performances of copyrighted songs, arrangements or recordings mentioned in this Play, the permission of the copyright owner(s) must be obtained. Other songs, arrangements or recordings may be substituted provided permission from the copyright owner(s) of such songs, arrangements or recordings is obtained; or songs, arrangements or recordings in the public domain may be substituted.

2

AUTHOR'S NOTE

In the play there is a great deal of overlapping dialogue which should be trigger-fired in its delivery. The *Jar* women have little time to listen to each other's truths and no time or patience for sentence punctuation. They are already busy forming a response, a counterattack if you will. In this vein, these women are not sentimental and fight ferociously against tears and other demonstrations of "precious" emotion; for one can never be weak in front of one's designated opponent. In this case, one's mother, one's daughter. And yet the love peeps through, always, even as the battle lines are drawn in fear and fury.

JAR THE FLOOR was originally produced by Parkland College in Champaign, Illinois, in 1989. It was directed by Cheryl L. West; the set design was by David Harwell; the lighting design was by Kathy Perkins; the sound design was by Carla Peyton; and the stage manager was Pamela Greer. The cast was as follows:

MADEAR	Ruth Latham
LOLA	Crystal Laws Green
MAYDEE	Margaret Porter-Wright
RAISA	Jackie Farber
VENNIE	Nonita Stiggers

JAR THE FLOOR received its professional premiere at the Empty Space Theatre (Kurt Beattie, Artistic Director; Melissa Hines, Managing Director) in Seattle, Washington, on June 12, 1991. It was directed by Gilbert McCauley; the set design was by Don Yanik; the costume design was by Sarah Campbell; the lighting design was by Brian Duea; the sound design was by David Pascal; and the stage manager was Linda Fane. The cast was as follows:

MADEAR	Tamu Gray
LOLA	Crystal Laws Green
MAYDEE	Jacqueline Moscou
RAISA	Laurie Thomas
VENNIE	Mari-Lynn

JAR THE FLOOR premiered in New York City at the Second Stage Theatre (Carole Rothman, Artistic Director; Christopher Burney, Associate Artistic Director; Carol Fishman, Managing Director; Alexander Fraser, Executive Director) on August 16, 1999. It was directed by Marion McClinton; the set design was by David Gallo; the lighting design was by Donald Holder; the sound design was by Janet Kalas; the costume design was by Michael Krass; the production stage manager was Diane DiVita; and the stage manager was Glynn David Turner. The cast was as follows:

MADEAR .... Irma P. Hall
LOLA .... Lynne Thigpen
MAYDEE .... Regina Taylor
RAISA .... Welker White
VENNIE .... Linda Powell

CHARACTERS

MADEAR — 90, mother of Lola, grandmother of MayDee and great-grandmother of Vennie.

LOLA — 65, daughter of MaDear, mother of MayDee and grandmother to Vennie.

MAYDEE — 47, daughter of Lola, mother of Vennie and granddaughter of MaDear.

VENNIE — 28, daughter of MayDee, granddaughter of Lola and great-granddaughter of MaDear.

RAISA — 30, friend of Vennie.

All the women are black, except Raisa, who is Jewish.

PLACE

MayDee Lakeland's house in Park Forest, Illinois, a middle-class suburb south of Chicago.

TIME

MaDear's ninetieth birthday.

JAR THE FLOOR

ACT ONE

Scene 1

Music and then in a dramatic light we see ninety-year-old MaDear wearing a flowing white gown that billows around her body as she studies herself in the mirror, the picture of complete stillness except for the graceful movement of the gown's material. Finally she moves, endeavoring to balance one foot and then the other. Eventually we realize she's attempting to dance, her arthritic limbs barely flexible; it's an act more deserving of pity than celebration.

MaDear laughs to herself, then turns up the nearby radio. A few more balancing movements but then suddenly MaDear slams her hand against the mirror. Sound of shattering glass. After a moment, an elegant yet frantic MayDee bursts into the room. She wears an expensive pajama and robe set — a woman of impeccable taste but at the moment thoroughly annoyed.

MAYDEE. What in heaven's name have you done this time? I can't even do my prayers in peace. *(Notices the cracked mirror.)* That's it. The next mirror you break in this house, I'm locking up every last one of them … *(MaDear turns the radio up to a blare, drowning out MayDee.)* Please turn that down. I'm trying to talk to you. Turn it down. *(Snatching the radio away.)* I said turn it

7

down. It's loud enough to wake the dead. *(Note that MayDee has a nervous habit of stretching out both her hands repeatedly.)*

MADEAR. *(Loudly.)* Man you woke?

MAYDEE. MaDear, I'm one exposed nerve, so please don't start that today, okay? *(MayDee sighs, kneels to pick up the broken glass, her back to MaDear. Nicks herself with a glass shard.)* Shoot! MaDear can you hand me a paper towel … *(No response. MayDee turns around and realizes MaDear is gone. She mutters an expletive, sucks the cut, then exits into the hallway that leads to the combined living room and kitchen. There is no sign of MaDear. She notices the exterior door open. She mutters another expletive and exits to find an agitated MaDear in the yard using her cane to shift dirt around a tree.)*

MADEAR. Planted my cabbage and rutabaga but ain't nuttin' taken root.

MAYDEE. That's because there's nothing there to root. I tell you this every morning. Now come back in the house. Please, MaDear. Come on. There's nothing planted out here but that old tree. Come on, sweetheart. Stop being a sight for the neighbors. *(Realizing they've been spotted by a neighbor.)* Oh Lord … *(MayDee assumes the false neighborly smile, waves to the neighbor.)* Yes, hello Mr. Cosine. *(Nervously clutching her nightgown in an effort to shield her modesty. MayDee turns her attention back to MaDear who is still looking for the nonexistent garden. The sight touches MayDee.)* MaDear, honey, if you come in the house, MayDee'll fix you breakfast. Mama'll be here soon to get you dolled up for your birthday … now come along … *(Taking in MaDear's disheveled hair.)* What is it that you do to your hair? *(MayDee leads MaDear into the house where MaDear eventually sits at the kitchen table and MayDee busies herself in the kitchen.)*

MADEAR. *(Overlapping.)* Don't like how dat gal plait. She know I's tender-headed an she catch my hair up an pull it so my eyes move way on de other side of my face …

MAYDEE. You only do that to your hair to upset Mama.

MADEAR. I cain't call dat gal's name. What name you say she go by again?

MAYDEE. Last I looked, you had one daughter MaDear. How come you can't remember her name? LOLA! *(Looks at the clock, then more to herself.)* What time do you think they'll call?

8

MADEAR. What?

MAYDEE. My tenure. I told you they were supposed to call today.

MADEAR. Chile, you talk so much I cain't keep up witcha.

MAYDEE. You think I deserve tenure, don't you? That I'm a good teacher ...

MADEAR. How I'm s'posed to know? If you gotta go askin me, it don't matter how good you is. Chile, fetch me my comb. Man's comin to git me today. Got to fix myself up, leave here lookin' decent ... Man don't like me lookin' old? Did you hear me MayDee? I'm goin' home. I'm goin' home ...

MAYDEE. How about something different this morning? An omelet, broccoli with mushrooms ...

MADEAR. Man don't eat no mushrooms, says it keeps yo bowels from formin up right, come out wid little hoods on 'em an sometimes dem hoods get caught and you needs you a button hook to try an pry 'em loose ...

MAYDEE. Okay, okay, MaDear, that's enough. No omelet. How about sausage and biscuits?

MADEAR. I don't eat no can biscuits made by no man name Hungry Jack.

MAYDEE. *(Firmly places a box of cereal and milk on the table.)* Knock yourself out. Now would you like a slice of melon?

MADEAR. It come out my garden?

MAYDEE. There's no garden, MaDear.

MADEAR. Well, you ain't killin me wid no store bought fruit and vege'bles. And where's my hog head cheese?

MAYDEE. How many times do I have to tell you they don't sell hog head cheese?

MADEAR. Den buy me a snout and I'll fix me some.

MAYDEE. *(Puts a slice of melon next to her bowl, cuts it up in little pieces.)* MaDear, today I would like you to try and stay sane. Understand? Sane! Can you do that for me? No talk about Papa, Man, Uncle. Nothing. You understand? *(Pulls up the window shade.)* Looks like Vennie will have a nice clear day in which to travel. I've made a lot of plans for this weekend. Did I show you the itinerary I had my secretary type up? It's going to be great, isn't it? You, me, Mama and of course my Vennie. *(MayDee hugs and*

9

kisses MaDear.)
MADEAR. You gon' kiss at me all day? *(During the next, MayDee takes out two liquor bottles and, while using a funnel, begins diluting the liquor with water.)*
MAYDEE. I sure hope that piece of car of Vennie's holds up.
MADEAR. Shouldn't bought no black car. If you gon' call yoself buyin a car, you might as well buy yoself a white one. I gots me a white car back home, big shiny white car.
MAYDEE. You don't have a white car, MaDear.
MADEAR. *(Overlapping, chuckling to herself imitates driving.)* I puts on my red hat and I drives it everywhere, everywhere I wanna go.
MAYDEE. MaDear, you don't have a white car or any other car. You never learned to drive.
MADEAR. Don't you tell me 'bout what I learnt. I used to teach school. Drive my white car every day to de schoolhouse.
MAYDEE. And you never taught school. You were never a teacher …
MADEAR. Chil'ren everywhere. Mornin' Miss Dawkins. Every mornin', dey say "mornin' Miss Dawkins" and I say "mornin' chil'ren … "
MAYDEE. There were no children, MaDear …
MADEAR. *(Overlapping.)* "Good mornin'." So don't tell me. Nuttin' a black car can do for me but carry me to a white one.
MAYDEE. MaDear I was talking about Vennie. Vennie and her car.
MADEAR. Who?
MAYDEE. VENNIE! YOUR GREAT-GRANDDAUGHTER!
MADEAR. Well chile, now you ain't gotta shout. Nuttin' wrong wid my hearin'. *(Yells.)* Man git Blackie. *(Starts taking off robe.)* Hitch up de wagon, we need to git on back home. We done stayed way too long in dis God-forsaken place …
MAYDEE. *(Exasperated.)* MaDear, remember that little lecture I gave you on staying sane? So let's keep that at the forefront. I tell you this every day, Papa's been dead nearly a year and then we brought you up here …
MADEAR. Gal, you sho is talkin silly. *(Throws her bowl on the floor, takes her cane and pounds the floor.)* Jar de floor man. You ain't dead. *(Grins to herself.)* You feel dat floor move? Don't you feel it? You hear him? Dat's the sweet sound of my man …

MAYDEE. *(Crossing to table, wipes up the floor.)* Oh MaDear ...

MADEAR. I said did you feel dat floor move? I cain't hardly hold myself in dis here chair, feel like I'm gon' fly away to Jesus. *(Laughs, then rakes her hand through MayDee's hair.)* Gal, you done pull most of yo hair out dere on de side, you nearly bald ...

MAYDEE. *(Hurt.)* Why would you say that? *(Going to the mirror.)* I just need another rinse.

MADEAR. Say rinse! Well, you can rinse if you want to, rinse yo hair right down de drain ... *(Lola enters through back door balancing bags and boxes overflowing with food and party decorations. At first glance, we know this is a women who does everything in excess, including her dress which is quite flashy but not totally at the expense of good taste.)*

LOLA. Morning my sweet darlings.

MADEAR. *(Muttering.)* And speakin of de drain ...

LOLA. How's everybody this fine God-sent beautiful morning? Hot as blue blazes out there. *(Kisses MayDee.)* Daughter, look like somebody walked on your face last night and left they tracks.

MAYDEE. *(Still studying her hair.)* Thanks Mama.

LOLA. *(Looking in the mirror behind MayDee.)* The right kind of color make that bald spot look like you got baby hair.

MAYDEE. What is this? I'm not going bald.

LOLA. It's okay baby. Your father was bald at twenty, head smooth as a baby's behind. Pretended he still had hair too. Used to scratch his bald head every Sunday afternoon, just like clockwork. And every Sunday afternoon I'd tell him his hair sho was growing. *(Suddenly dry.)* Morning Mama.

MADEAR. None of dem Smith boys ever had any hair. Heard tell dey didn't have hair no wheres 'bout dey body, not a lick.

LOLA. And where'd you hear that from Mama?

MADEAR. Don't you worry 'bout where missy.

LOLA. Well, they told you a lie. That man was hairy like a gorilla. I never knew if I was having a nightmare or if it was just Smith turning over trying to get him a little bit. I'm so thankful baby you didn't come here looking like a little monkey; I'd been shaving your whole body every single day, thank you Jesus! *(Starts taking things out of her bag.)* Now quit fretting MayDee. You lose all your hair, just buy yourself a wig and keep on stepping. It's a

11

sin to be so vain. I don't know where you get that from. *(Handing her some plastic containers.)* Here put this cole slaw in the 'frigerator and here the beans ... candied yams ...

MADEAR. Hair is a woman's glory.

LOLA. And that's a white woman's lie. By the time a colored woman get through rinsing, coloring, straightening, yanking, greasing that kitchen, trying to tame her some hair, she done gone to glory and back. I bet if you go to heaven right now, there'd be a bunch of nappy-headed black angels laughing their butts off singing free at last, free at last ...

MAYDEE. Mama!

LOLA. I'm tryin' to tell you the God's honest truth. We all gon' end up looking like them Jamaican mountain people before it's over. Saw it in a dream once. I fried some chicken too. Here. Don't put it in the 'frigerator, just leave it on the stove ...

MAYDEE. You didn't have to do all this cooking ...

LOLA. Yes I did.

MAYDEE. I was going to make a pot roast ...

LOLA. When?

MAYDEE. For dinner.

LOLA. And you ain't got on it yet?

MAYDEE. There's still time ...

LOLA. I didn't wanna eat at midnight, that's why I went on 'head and cooked. Anyway my Pick-Me-Up like chicken better than pot roast ... And what time that child getting here?

MAYDEE. Some time this morning. *(Bringing Lola her special house shoes.)* There are several lectures this evening on campus I thought she might enjoy. Perhaps a movie. And tomorrow I thought we'd go to an art exhibition after brunch ... then maybe to the ...

LOLA. So what time you schedule her to shit? That child is grown, MayDee. You need to stop planning her life out like that.

MAYDEE. I don't.

LOLA. Fine. I ain't in it. You like this little purse?

MAYDEE. Un-hun.

LOLA. It's a Louis Vuitton.

MAYDEE. It's nice.

LOLA. *(Crossing to couch, lights a cigarette.)* You think so? I think

12

it's the ugliest thing. But all my clubwomen buyin' 'em, trying to buy 'em some class. *(MayDee brings her an ashtray.)* And you know Alberta, she had to go and outdo everybody. Went and bought herself a big-ass briefcase and don't put nothing in it but bananas.

MAYDEE. Bananas?

LOLA. Yeah, she eats 'em round the clock for her potassium. You know who she is, look like a little haint. And ain't nuttin' worse than a haint trying to be siddity! And how the hell you gon' be siddity when you buy your shoes and food at the same store ... now tell me that! That woman needed a briefcase like she needed a hole in her head. A Louis Vuitton with bananas in it! She won't even keep the minutes at the meetings. I told her she oughtta be the secretary; at least she'd have reason to carry that thing around. But no, told me she done retired from a women's work. Ain't that something? She done retired! I told her every time she lay on her back underneath that ton of fun she married to, she doing a woman's work. *(Holds up the purse.)* Ain't big enough to hold nothing but some Kleenex and some small change. Paid all that money just to hold Kleenex. *(MayDee exits.)*

MADEAR. How much you pay for dat bag, Sister?

LOLA. Ninety-five, I think.

MADEAR. Gal is you silly? Hope it was ninety-five cents. A pillowcase been prettier.

LOLA. Glad I didn't buy you one.

MADEAR. You and me both happy 'bout dat.

LOLA. Aw, close your legs, Mama. *(Yelling toward hallway.)* MayDee, I don't know why you let her sit around here all day long with her legs wide open.

MADEAR. Dey my legs. And dey don't close up no mo. *(Fans her robe.)* My air is findin its way.

LOLA. Your what? *(Closes MaDear's legs.)* Them legs would close if you wanted them to. AND KEEP YOUR HANDS FROM DOWN THERE. Ain't nuttin' down there still requirin' your attention. *(MayDee enters, sprays the room with air spray. Attempt at nonchalance to MayDee.)* Anybody call?

MAYDEE. Who are you expecting this time?

LOLA. That's my business, dear heart.

MAYDEE. I told you before, my phone is not your answering service.

LOLA. I know that, sweetheart.

MAYDEE. Then why don't you have your so-called "dates" ...

LOLA. Hush up. You know I don't want her knowing my business ...

MADEAR. Wouldn't be caught doin' nuttin' I had to talk down to de floor 'bout.

LOLA. I swear she could hear a chinch piss on cotton. *(Yelling to MaDear.)* To be ninety, you got good hearing, old woman. *(To MayDee.)* You sure your phone is working? I knew I should've called and checked it out but you know how mine go in and out. That's why I got to look my spanking best, day and night. No telling when my number is gon' be up living in that shack. That's why I'm so grateful Mama is here with you. It's so much safer!

MAYDEE. Boy, that's a new one.

LOLA. What?

MAYDEE. You don't live in a shack ...

LOLA. Well, if I lived in a mansion like this, there would be no problem ...

MAYDEE. Three bedrooms is hardly a mansion and please, Mama, you own an entire building. Any one of those apartments you could have moved MaDear in or she could have stayed with you.

LOLA. Just cause I'm on a fixed income, you trying to make me feel bad. How 'bout that brother of mine? You don't see him volunteering to take her. He living up there in that fancy house with that no English-speaking wife that never shuts up ... you know anybody that talk more than me, ain't doing nuttin' but lying ...

MADEAR. Doctor don't have no wife. He's comin for me.

LOLA. He ain't comin' for you and he's ain't a doctor, Mama. Shit. He runs a maid service. He's a pimp in the cleaning business.

MAYDEE. Please, don't start. Not today. If she wants to believe ...

LOLA. No. Un-un. She don't allow me my lies, so why should I allow her hers? I get sick of you calling him the Doctor. His name is A.H. He ain't no M.D. He liked to cut up animals and that's as far as his medical training went.

MADEAR. Gal, how you know? You ain't never been to my house.

14

LOLA. Here we go. Which doorstep did you find me on today?

MAYDEE. *(Unwraps a piece of candy.)* You know I really wish you'd stop giving my number out.

LOLA. *(Overlapping, takes the candy from MayDee's mouth.)* Give me that, your behind getting too big now ... *(Eats the candy.)*

MAYDEE. I just wish you'd settle down with someone your own age ...

LOLA. Settle! *(Gesturing toward MaDear.)* That's what settle looks like and I sho ain't ready for that.

MAYDEE. You'd rather chase after these boys? Let them use you as a business ...

LOLA. Better used than going to waste. MayDee, don't you miss having somebody to hold, make you feel like a woman?

MAYDEE. Mama, I don't want to hold on to something I know can't handle the weight. I'm content ...

LOLA. Content?! What about being happy?

MAYDEE. I've always preferred the ease of contentment to the strife of happiness.

LOLA. Now that don't even make sense. I can't talk to you when you talking through them degrees of yours. There's no substitute for a good man ...

MAYDEE. Then learn to masturbate. It's safer, cleaner and more expedient.

LOLA. And why don't you shut your filthy mouth.

MADEAR. Better a filthy mouth den a filthy behind.

LOLA. Mama, Lola and MayDee talking. Understand? This an 'A-B' conversation so 'C' your way out of it.

MAYDEE. *(Overlapping.)* Somebody your own age, like Mr. Brown. You two look so cute ...

LOLA. MayDee, I left cute when I started walking.

MADEAR. You never walked. You went straight from crawlin' to switchin' yo behind.

LOLA. Yeah, I did have a walk, didn't I? Stop traffic. And dance oh my land. Could've gone professional. *(Demonstrating.)* Should've seen me kicking high, high, high at the Club DeLisa. Yes ma'am, star quality. The Parkway Ballroom, the RhumBoogie ... Sometimes I'd go seven days a week. Back then folks in Chicago didn't know what a bad time was ... and dress ooh look out! You ain't seen such pretty. And your Mama was hangin' right there with 'em. I'd put on my high heels and my stink-stink and I stepped out smellin' better and lookin' better than anybody's rich white folks ... Yes, Lord ... I'm tryin to tell you about the real truth! Come on dance with me, MayDee. Dance with your old mother. *(Starts dancing.)*

MAYDEE. Mama, it's too early to be dancing.

LOLA. It's never too early. Dancing don't need no time permit. I got up this morning dancing. *(She swings MayDee around.)* Why don't you tickle them ivories a little?

MAYDEE. You know I don't play anymore.

LOLA. *(Plays a few keys on the piano.)* Just a few notes, baby.

MAYDEE. I said no.

LOLA. Okay, then just dance with me ... *(Lola swings MayDee again and then gets caught up in her own rhythm; MayDee watches her appreciatively as Lola sings.)* "Whatever Lola wants, Lola gets ... and little man, little Lola wants you ... Jump back honey, jump back. Watch me now. Jump back honey, jump back." *(Dancing over to MaDear.)* Come on, Mama, you wanna dance?

MADEAR. You better git away from me gal wid all dat mess. You better git somewhere an find de Lord.

LOLA. *(Deflated.)* You just can't let me be free. Between you and the Lord it's a wonder I'm able to greet the sun every morning.

MADEAR. You little split-tail, don't you blaspheme de Lord.

MAYDEE. You're a wonderful dancer, Mama ... always have been ...

LOLA. *(Catching her breath, rubbing her feet.)* I used to pop my dress and now I can barely pop my fingers. I'd still be dancing regular if my feet weren't so bad ...

MAYDEE. But Mr. Brown doesn't seem to mind.

LOLA. How you know what he minds?

MAYDEE. He adores you Mama. You took that cruise together and he's a man of independent means. Your own age ... Why don't you invite him over today for the party?

LOLA. What is he paying you or what?! His name been chasing out your mouth ever since I walked through that door.

MAYDEE. I just think ...

LOLA. MayDee, I don't know how many times I have to tell you

16

but there's a devil in every detail.

MAYDEE. And what does that have to do with Mr. Brown, Mama?

LOLA. *(Feigned nonchalance.)* I really can't say.

MAYDEE. Come on, Mama ...

LOLA. Didn't I say I couldn't say? *(Crosses away from MaDear, whispering.)* They gave your Mr. Brown the zipper cut. Balls gone ... over and out!

MAYDEE. Mama, he had prostate surgery. They didn't cut his testicles off.

LOLA. Well it ain't like I looked. We keep good company but I ain't ready to get my pleasure through no rub-a-dub-dub. I like something with a little more substance. You know what I mean? *(Laughs.)*

MAYDEE. No.

LOLA. Shit, MayDee, you been running on empty too long. There's no rising in the flour. You understand now? *(Makes gesture.)* NO RISING!

MAYDEE. *(Laughing.)* Oh Mama!

LOLA. I'm telling you the God's honest truth, the candle ain't matching the flame, baby! He wants to kiss and kiss, kiss ... slobber ... kiss ... slobber. My whole body being baptized with his mouth. And you know me, I don't go in for no freaky-deaky ...

MAYDEE. At least he's affectionate. You can't ask for more than that.

LOLA. Yeah, he's affectionate all right, but so is a blanket if you wrap it right. *(Catches MaDear eavesdropping.)* Mama, why don't you go and get your clothes laid out.

MADEAR. Ain't wearin' no clothes today.

LOLA. Well, then why don't you go watch TV in your room?

MADEAR. Ain't watchin' no TV today.

LOLA. Then go in your room and just sit there. I'll be in directly to get you cleaned up and comb that head, look like the chickens been playing in it again.

MADEAR. I'm fine where I is. I ain't no child dats got to be sent to my room. *(Lola crosses, turns on the TV, then moves with some effort MaDear's chair closer to the TV; it takes a lot of effort since MaDear doesn't help in the least bit, even drags her feet.)*

17

MAYDEE. I wish you all would stop moving that chair.

LOLA. When my surprise comes, we won't have to do this.

MAYDEE. What surprise? Mama, would you put that chair back? You're scratching the floor …

LOLA. It looks better here. Gives the room a lived in effect and Lord knows this room could use some personality … And you might as well sell that piano, nothing but a dust collector. *(To MaDear.)* Now sweetie, you watch a little TV while me and MayDee talk. Okay? *(MaDear doesn't respond. Lola crosses to kitchen area and as soon as she starts talking to MayDee, MaDear uses the remote to click off the TV but continues to stare at it as if it's on, all the while listening to their conversation. Periodically she looks over at them.)* I needs me some coffee.

MAYDEE. I'm not sure I want to hear this.

LOLA. You got anything in that bottom cabinet?

MAYDEE. It's a little early, don't you think?

LOLA. Yeah, we having us a morning drink. *(Retrieving the "doctored" liquor bottle from the cabinet, pours some in her cup.)* Coffee is for morning, we just stirring a little evening in it.

MAYDEE. Go ahead. Let's hear this. I can hardly wait.

LOLA. What I'm gon' tell you is gon' shock every bit of shit outta you. Gon' give you an enema right here on the spot.

MAYDEE. *(Laughing.)* I doubt it Mama, but go ahead.

LOLA. Brace yourself. I hate to tell you this about your Mr. Brown, but he wanted me to do an unnatural act.

MAYDEE. Now this is getting good.

LOLA. Yes. Told me other women have no hesitation. Even had a magazine … living color with the shit in it.

MAYDEE. Uh-hun.

LOLA. He wanted me to … Lord Jesus my throat is closing up a mile a minute just thinking about it. I'm so shamed.

MAYDEE. Mama, are you trying to tell me he wanted you to have oral sex?

LOLA. Ooh, honey, don't say it out loud!

MAYDEE. *(Laughs.)* It's just an alternative Mama. Myself, I happen to enjoy it better than intercourse.

LOLA. SHUT YOUR MOUTH AND THROW AWAY THE KEY!

MAYDEE. I'm serious. I can count the times on one hand where I've achieved orgasm through intercourse.

LOLA. Well, you ain't gon' catch me achieving that shit. I told him my mouth was a sanctuary, you hear me, a sanctuary! I couldn't have no man smelling me all up in my privates, all your fare the well wide open, exposed. And let's face it, pussy ain't pretty.

MAYDEE. Really? I think it's quite beautiful.

LOLA. Lord Jesus I'm getting dizzy. *(Getting up.)* I knew you was educated but I didn't know you was doing the freaky. *(Opens a window to get some air.)* Shoot, you done given me a serious hot flash.

MADEAR. Wouldn't have no sin I had to pay for. And he's my husband!

LOLA. Mama, what you talking about?

MADEAR. *(Overlapping.)* He's my husband, not yo husband. You hear dat split tail? He's mine! My husband.

LOLA. Mama, stop talking silly ...

MAYDEE. Could we all try and get along, at least for the day?

LOLA. I was trying, but she talking 'bout somebody's husband ...

MAYDEE. Just for the day. Okay? Okay?

LOLA. *(Reluctantly.)* Okay. Okay. Okay already! *(Crossing to MaDear, false gaiety.)* And how's the birthday girl this morning? *(Kissing MaDear.)*

MADEAR. Every time you kiss me wid dem red lips I gits me a rash. Why I got to pay for yo sins?

LOLA. Nobody asked you to pay for a damn ...

MAYDEE. *(Interceding, swirls to model the robe.)* Mama, you like this robe? I got it on sale at Saks ...

LOLA. I don't know why you spend good money on stuff like that. It's not like you're wearing it for anybody. Come on. Let me show you all the things I got for the party. You wanna see, Mama? You wanna see the sign I made? *(Retrieves a huge banner decorated "Happy Birthday," Lola-style.)* You like it, Mama? *(No response, nor does she look at the sign.)* Did you hear me? *(Irritated.)* Mama, do you like the sign? It says happy birthday.

MADEAR. I can read.

MAYDEE. She likes it, don't you MaDear?

MADEAR. De Doctor sent me a blue dress.

LOLA. He sent you that dress six months ago. *(Disgustedly dropping the sign.)*

MAYDEE. It's a nice dress just like this sign Mama made for you.

MADEAR. He's comin' for me. My boy was sho nuff a gift from God.

LOLA. *(Pours another drink.)* Good thing God gave him to you, nobody else would've wanted him. *(The phone rings. MayDee and Lola freeze.)*

LOLA. Well, aren't you going to answer it?

MAYDEE. Maybe it's for you.

LOLA. It's not my house.

MAYDEE. So! That never mattered before.

LOLA. Well, I ain't one for answering other people's phones.

MADEAR. WILL ONE OF Y'ALL ANSWER DE DAMN PHONE!

MAYDEE. *(Hesitates, pick up the phone, is shaky with anticipation.)* Hello? *(Registers her disappointment; it's not who she had hoped it would be.)* Oh … yes operator I will … *(MaDear starts talking to herself. What she says is not really audible, but clearly she's having a running conversation with herself or her imagination, it's a conversation with intense emotional range.)*

MAYDEE. *(In the phone.)* Vennie, what are you doing calling here? I expected you to be pulling in the driveway …

LOLA. *(Overlapping.)* Tell her don't tie up that phone. Your bill too high now, her calling and reversing them charges from all over the country …

MAYDEE. Well, it's a fine time to tell me … she's welcome, that's not the point …

LOLA. Who? Who?

MAYDEE. Okay … Can you tell me now? Vennie, I would just like a little preparation … Vennie, who do you think you're talking … fine … fine … See you when you get here. *(Hangs up.)*

LOLA. Who she bringing?

MAYDEE. A friend.

LOLA. Female?

MAYDEE. It appears so. I know Vennie, she just didn't decide to bring somebody … this is her M-O. She wants something. Said she had something important to discuss. All this secrecy. She

20

couldn't tell me on the phone ... Nooo, she has to wait until she gets here ...

LOLA. With a friend.

MAYDEE. I've made reservations. I hadn't planned on an extra person ...

LOLA. An extra female person. Don't mean no harm MayDee, she's your daughter and my granddaughter and I love her dearly, but I'm beginning to wonder about our Vennie, my little Pick-Me-Up. She like women a little too much, don't you think? Catch my drift?

MAYDEE. I'm glad she likes women. Means she likes herself.

LOLA. I likes myself too but I don't like no women! Shoot! 'Member that time I caught her with that Johnson gal, both of 'em holding their dresses up, their little rabbits sticking out. Now, I didn't stay 'round to see what else they was 'bout to do ... but if you ask me ...

MAYDEE. Mama, she was ten years old!

LOLA. Ten and on fire. That stuff start in you young and once it gets started ... whew! Look out. I read where that stuff courses through your veins till your blood even change up.

MAYDEE. Changes up to what, Mama?

LOLA. *(At a lost for a minute.)* Well I didn't watch the whole program. But I 'member you start growing hair everywhere, little beards.

MAYDEE. Mama, you have a beard.

LOLA. *(As if she's been slapped, beyond furious.)* That's a bald face lie! Where? I got tweezers in hand day and night! You don't tell me. Sometimes I have a basin full of hair, plucking. Shoot! Just cause you don't want to admit the truth you gon' try and detour me talking 'bout my face.

MAYDEE. Mama, what truth? Whatever Vennie is doing or not doing about her sexuality is really not my concern at the moment. If I know Vennie she's just as likely to be cohabiting with a feather next week.

LOLA. And mark my words, it'll be a female feather! *(MayDee laughs.)* Go 'head. Make fun, but when you get old and don't have no little grandbabies running around, you'll be sorry ... you'll be sorry you didn't let her have that baby.

MAYDEE. Mama, could you please tell me how you went from

21

the hair on your face to Vennie's decision not to have a baby? Could you please explain that connection?

LOLA. The connection is a baby sets you on the straight and narrow path. Ain't no detouring with nobody's female feathers. You's a mother and you knows you's a woman! Your life is mapped out. Ain't that right Mama?

MADEAR. I have to go to de bafroom.

LOLA. Then take your behind in there.

MADEAR. Gal, I should've killed you when you was born.

MAYDEE. *(Assisting MaDear.)* MaDear, come on I'll help you. *(MaDear exits.)* Do you have to antagonize her like that? You know she can't help herself. I think she's getting a touch of Alzheimer's.

LOLA. Hmph! Lie-heimers you mean! Mama got more sense than the two of us put together. Stayed up, cooked, made that silly sign, bought all that food and decorations so she could have a good birthday. Does she appreciate it? Noooo. *(Yells toward the direction of the bathroom.)* DOES SHE APPRECIATE ALL I DO FOR HER? HAS SHE EVER APPRECIATED ANYTHING I EVER DID?

MAYDEE. I'm so tired of starting my mornings like this. It's either the radio blasting, broken glass, her yelling and then there's your daily visit.

LOLA. Well sir, I been put out of better places than this. I don't have to come here. I call myself trying to help out. I come, give her a bath, comb her hair and try to help out as best I can while you at that big shot job teaching black people how to be black.

MAYDEE. Mama, I teach African-American Studies and Political Science ...

LOLA. Call it what you want, but don't forget I sit here all day long, every day, playing nursemaid to somebody who'd rather die than act like I'm in the same room. Every day! From now on, I'll just keep my black ass home ...

MAYDEE. Are you just oblivious? Do you know the stress I'm under? My hair is falling out ... I'm working around the clock, I have a grandmother who'd make Jesus Christ cry out for mercy ... and I'm waiting on one of the biggest decisions of my life ... Of course you wouldn't care ...

22

LOLA. *(Dramatically pitiful.)* She's turned you against me, hasn't she?

MAYDEE. *(Straightening up the house.)* Can't do this today.

LOLA. She told me I wasn't gon' be no kinda mother. But I did the best I could, kept you clean, kept a man, even when I didn't want one, so you'd have a father ...

MAYDEE. Thanks.

LOLA. Now what was that smart-aleck remark for?

MAYDEE. Nothing.

LOLA. Don't tell me nothing. Every child needs a father. Wouldn't've known how to laugh without mine. Maybe Willie or Sam or Joe weren't the best fathers.

MAYDEE. Can say that again.

LOLA. At least they were there ... more than I can say for that father who planted you in me. He never gave you a dime, not one red cent ...

MAYDEE. I guess you think having four fathers is some type of blessing.

LOLA. At least they loved you. Willie wanted to legally adopt you, 'member? But I told him no out of respect for your real father.

MAYDEE. Can we talk about something else? Please? *(Busies herself with yet another household chore, anything to block out Lola's drone.)*

LOLA. *(Overlapping.)* Willie was always taking up time, playing your little games with you. That man loved you ... more than I thought he loved me sometimes. I used to feel so left out around the two of y'all. Just hang in the doorway grinning till my mouth got all dried out, waiting for y'all to notice me. What was that one game you never got tired of ... used to sit on his knee and he'd bounce you up and down and y'all would clap hands ... *(Sings and claps her hands.)* "Little pretty May, pretty as a picture ... "

MAYDEE. I don't remember.

LOLA. Oh, yes you do. You would clap ... *(Sings, claps her hands.)* "Nuttin' like her Mama cause she daddy's little girl, pretty as a picture, makes her Daddy ... "

MAYDEE. Would you like to see the outfit I bought for Vennie?

LOLA. *(Overlapping.)* I remember I had to tell him to stop playing with you like that ...

23

MAYDEE. *(Overlapping.)* I probably paid too much for it ...

LOLA. *(Overlapping.)* You was going on fifteen and he still thought you liked that game ... *(Laughing at the memory.)* Was scared all that bouncing up and down was gon' ruin your figure. Never did have much up there, I didn't want what you had to start dropping down.

MAYDEE. And a woman is nothing without a good figure, right? Maybe if you had been any kind of mother then maybe I wouldn't have needed a father so damn much.

LOLA. *(Momentarily shocked.)* Why you cutting me to pieces today, huh MayDee? Just butchering my heart left and right.

MAYDEE. It's like you don't even hear me. Did you hear me say my future hangs in the air? I'm not waiting for some gigolo stud to call ... I'm waiting on something I've worked my whole life for.

LOLA. And I've worked my whole life for a good man ...

MAYDEE. I give up. You've always been so self-involved ... you don't see anything beyond your own narcissistic reality.

LOLA. Well, you forgive me for my *(Tries to say the word, gets tangled in the pronunciation.)* narcis ... narcis ... whatever the shit you called it. You try walking a mile on the roads I traveled. You try cleaning up behind white folks everyday and coming home to a daughter who you can't buy a smile from and a nigger who acts like you ain't even there ...

MAYDEE. Your choice. Not mine. Yours.

LOLA. I didn't have a choice. You had to eat.

MAYDEE. Right.

LOLA. Show me a woman who's never had to spread her legs, who didn't have to lay down somewheres first so she could rise up later with a loaf of bread in hand.

MAYDEE. I never did.

LOLA. Well good for you, Miss Thang! And while you feeling so superior try remembering how I kept your belly full, how you had a roof over your head ... that you wore decent clothes ... had toys, your own piano.

MAYDEE. I just want you to stop using me ... stop making me sorry for being born.

LOLA. I ain't never made you sorry for being born. God, how did I raise a goddamn sponge for a daughter? Soak up every misery in the world and squeeze it right back in my face. I can't help it that you've spoiled Vennie silly … that you think every man comes dipped in horseshit, that you work like a dog and there's nobody there to slap you on the back twenty-four hours a day. You want a backslapper MayDee, here, buy yourself one. *(Opens her purse, takes out some bills.)* I'll even throw in a few dollars and furnish you with a few names. *(Slaps the bills in MayDee's hands.)*

MAYDEE. I have to go help your mother. *(MayDee starts to exit. Lola grabs her.)*

LOLA. *(Pleading.)* MayDee wait, I do the best I can … You can't keep faulting me for doing the best I can. I know you the best thing ever came out of my life … God knows you are. *(MayDee throws the money at Lola's feet, exits.)* You waiting for this tenure, I'm waiting for this gigolo, different prize MayDee, but the need's the same.

Scene 2

Several hours later. In the dark we hear the sound of piano playing. Finally we see MayDee at the piano dramatically playing a classic, maybe from Beethoven, Bach. MaDear is in her chair dressed in the blue flowered dress. Her hair is neatly braided and pinned on top of her head. She watches MayDee in appreciation.

LOLA. *(After a time, off, yelling.)* Somebody help me. My arms 'bout to fall off. MayDee.

MAYDEE. *(Quickly shuts the piano, to MaDear.)* Remember this is our little secret. Sometimes I still need to see if the piano still works. *(MaDear nods agreeably, even manages a smile for MayDee.)*

LOLA. MAYDEE!

MAYDEE. I'm coming. *(Lola enters wheeling an electric wheelchair that is overflowing with packages, including a large framed mirror. She has changed clothes; the outfit is outlandish, red and complete*

25

with a glittery shawl or matching boa.)

LOLA. Whew, better stay young MayDee, getting old is a bitch.

MAYDEE. Mama, what in the world…?

LOLA. Vennie not here yet? I get my call?

MAYDEE. No. What is that?

LOLA. It's for Mama.

MAYDEE. Well, I knew it wasn't for me.

LOLA. Did I hear the piano? *(MayDee shakes her head no.)* And I took a mirror off my wall so you can stop complaining about all the mirrors she breaks …

MAYDEE. Mama, why in the world did you buy MaDear a wheel chair, and an electric one at that?

MADEAR. *(Overlapping.)* What's dat you got dere Sister?

LOLA. *(Takes packages out of chair.)* Here take these MayDee. I got a surprise for you Mama. *(Getting in the wheelchair, demonstrates.)* An electric wheelchair. All you have to do is push this here button and you can ride till your behind gets tired. *(Does a wheelie, gleefully.)* Yee-haw! Ride em Lola. Shoot, I might keep this thing myself.

MAYDEE. *(Jumping out of the way.)* Mama, I don't believe you did this.

LOLA. What?

MAYDEE. What? Buying her a wheelchair, that's what!

LOLA. I didn't buy it, I rented it.

MAYDEE. But MaDear can walk. You're going to make her cripple before her time.

LOLA. I thought it would help out. Make her more independent. *(Getting up.)* Come on Mama, try it out. Get in.

MAYDEE. *(Overlapping.)* Help out? This house isn't big enough for another piece of furniture.

LOLA. But it folds up MayDee. Got a little horn on it. Put it on myself. *(Lola squeezes the horn; it's an obnoxious sound.)*

MAYDEE. Do you see how narrow that hall is? That wheelchair will block this whole hall … all I need now is to add a traffic jam to my morning routine. My walls are still reeling from your last escapade … the crayons you bought her. Remember that? Remember my painting bill? *(On the last, MaDear loses control and the wheelchair careens straight into MayDee. MayDee winces in pain. Both*

26

MaDear and Lola freeze waiting for MayDee's explosion but none is forthcoming.)

LOLA. *(Sheepishly.)* MayDee, honey, Mama didn't mean to … Baby, are you hurt? You want Mama to kiss it and make it all better. *(MayDee gestures for Lola to freeze. Promptly turning on MaDear.)* Now who told you to turn this thing on? You done hurt MayDee so bad she can't even talk. Why you have to be so fast? I was gon' show you how to operate it …

MADEAR. I knows how to do. I knows how to drive.

LOLA. The only thing you ever drove was Papa, drove him crazy!

MADEAR. You de one dat drove him crazy. Killed him wid all dat dancin'.

MAYDEE. See what you've started. A wheelchair! Mama, I don't believe you.

LOLA. I was just trying to do something nice for her birthday. Every damn thing I do turns to piss … *(Attempts to light a cigarette.)*

MAYDEE. *(Waving the air.)* I wish you wouldn't do that in here.

LOLA. Why don't you say what you really mean? Mama I wish you'd disappear.

MAYDEE. *(A moment.)* Mama. *(No response.)* Mama, look … it was a nice thought but …

MADEAR. Nice way to kill a soul. A motor chair …

MAYDEE. I'm sorry. You're right, it's MaDear's birthday. Let's not ruin things. *(Lola doesn't respond.)* I know … Let me show you the new outfit I bought for Vennie. *(Goes in the closet, retrieves a suit on a hanger, shows it to Lola.)* You like it?

LOLA. Vennie's not gon' wear that shit.

MAYDEE. This suit cost me a lot of money.

LOLA. Is that why you left the price on? Take the tags off MayDee.

MAYDEE. What if I have to take it back? What if it doesn't fit?

LOLA. Cut the tags off, MayDee. I'll tell Vennie how much you paid for it.

MAYDEE. She's coming here for money. I can feel it.

LOLA. It's her money.

MAYDEE. It most certainly is not. I saved every last dime of that money. And I'm not giving up one red cent until she finishes … *(Catches herself.)*

LOLA. Finishes what?

MAYDEE. That money is for her to further her education.

LOLA. For what? She done got one degree. You aiming her toward a MD when what she needs is a J-O-B! You oughtta be tired of supporting her behind ...

MAYDEE. *(Overlapping, deliberately changes the subject.)* Why don't I just go hang this mirror in MaDear's room. *(Awkwardly handling the heavy mirror.)* Can you explain to me why you have to choose the biggest things all the time?

LOLA. *(Smiling to herself.)* Are we talking about men or furniture? *(Immediately jumping to her feet, follows MayDee down the hallway.)* Wait, that's my damn mirror!

MAYDEE. But it's my house.

LOLA. But it's my mother's room. Don't you drop my damn mirror. *(They exit and lights shift to outside where we see Vennie at the top of the tree drinking a beer and smoking a joint. Her head wrapped, she is especially decorated from head to toe with assorted piercings and tattoos.)*

RAISA. *(Off.)* Vennie, we got a flat tire. Vennie, did you hear me...? *(No response from Vennie. Instead Vennie takes another hit and another swig. Finally ...)*

VENNIE. I'm up in my tree.

RAISA. *(Entering. Raisa has noticeably one breast. She too has an odd sense of style and color)* What are you doing up there? Did you hear me say the front tire is flat?

VENNIE. Why you trippin'? We won't even need a car soon.

RAISA. I'm trippin' but you're the one smoking a joint in your mother's backyard.

VENNIE. Girl, let me try one more time to explain something to you. Weed is a necessary family prophylactic. It's the American way ... it's okay to go home but make sure you take a hit first and in my family, you need a big hit 'cause they'll have you sucking on a seed trying to get high ... *(Raisa laughs.)* You think I'm kidding, don't you?

RAISA. No, what I think is, you're stalling.

VENNIE. Okay, one more pass at the rules first.

RAISA. Compliment your grandmother on how young she looks.

VENNIE. Good.

RAISA. And debate politics with your mother.

VENNIE. Go to the head of the class ...

RAISA. And then your great-grandmother ... Vennie, I'm not going to remember all of this ...

VENNIE. Take a picture of me.

RAISA. Now?

VENNIE. Yeah. *(Posing dramatically.)*

RAISA. *(Getting the camera out.)* Vennie, I swear. *(She takes the picture.)*

VENNIE. I can't tell you how many hours I spent in this tree. This is where I wrote my first song. *(Lights shift and we see MayDee looking out the window.)*

MAYDEE. *(Overlapping, eyeing Raisa.)* My God ... Why today, Vennie? Why? *(The inside and outside scenes continue to overlap.)*

RAISA. *(Overlapping.)* Well why don't you write a song in the house? Where's the front door?

VENNIE. Okay, I'm coming down. *(Raisa and Vennie exit to the front of the house.)*

LOLA. *(Overlapping, off, yelling.)* Dammit MayDee! This mirror was 'bout to fall on my damn head. *(Entering.)* If you aim to kill me, just do it straight out. I don't wanna meet my maker with a mirror sticking out my forehead ... I'm telling you the truth ... What you looking at so? *(Trying hard to see but MayDee is ushering her away from the window.)* She got her friend with her?

MAYDEE. *(Overlapping.)* Yes. Now Mama, don't say anything to hurt Vennie's feelings. And no comments about her friend. You too MaDear.

MADEAR. I ain't gotta talk no mo today.

RAISA. *(Appearing outside the front door.)* It's a beautiful house from what I can see.

VENNIE. Remember to mention that to my mother. Oh no, where's the present?

MADEAR. Yes, I'm gon' sit right here in dis here motor chair.

LOLA. Well, I'm glad you like it Mama.

RAISA. *(Searching in her knapsack.)* Hold on I have it. *(Raisa retrieves an African coffee table book.)*

MADEAR. I don't 'member sayin' I liked it.

LOLA. *(To MayDee.)* This must really be bad, you stalling like this. Where's my drink? I need a drink before I see this God for-

29

saken child. She must look a sight.

VENNIE. Where's the bow? *(Raisa hands Vennie a huge bow.)* I don't remember it looking this big in the store ... *(Sticks it on the book.)* How's that look?

RAISA. Desperate.

LOLA. Me and Mama gon' sit here like two peas in a pod.

MADEAR. *(Crosses her arms too.)* Two no-talkin' peas.

LOLA. That's right, Mama.

VENNIE. Okay, let's see we got everything? *(Raisa takes mints out of her purse ... hands one to her.)*

MAYDEE. *(Overlapping.)* Remember, not a word ...

LOLA. *(Overlapping.)* Not one word gon' pass through these lips, not one damn word. I ain't gon' say shit to neither one of 'em, just watch me.

MADEAR. Watch me too. I'm tired of talkin'.

RAISA: Okay, I'm tired of this insanity. No more rules, no more rehearsal, no more stalling. I'm just going to be myself. *(She rings the doorbell.)*

MAYDEE. *(Overlapping.)* Okay, I'm opening the door.

LOLA. Oh don't be so dramatic, MayDee, open the goddamn door. Now close your legs, Mama. *(Puts her arms around MaDear's knees, tries to hold them closed.)*

MADEAR. Gal, take yo hands offa my legs.

MAYDEE. *(Giving them one more warning look before opening the door.)* Well, look who we have here. You finally made it.

VENNIE. Yeah, we finally made it.

MADEAR. *(Overlapping.)* MAN IT'S A PURE WHITE WOMAN! *(Clasps her hand over her mouth while Lola remains speechless.)*

VENNIE. This is for you. *(Handing MayDee the book.)*

MAYDEE. Well, this is some bow.

VENNIE. Yeah, I knew you would like it. Did you get your call?

MAYDEE. Not yet. Vennie, it appears you're using your body as a pincushion. When exactly did you decide to reinvent yourself?

VENNIE. Probably the last time I was home.

RAISA. *(Extending her hand to MayDee.)* Hi. I'm Raisa. You have a beautiful home, Mrs. Lakeland.

VENNIE. Yeah Mother, this is my friend Raisa.

MAYDEE. Hello. Ra-za …

RAISA. Raisa.

MAYDEE. *(Trying not to stare.)* That's a pretty name. Well, put your things down. Make yourself at home, Raisa. It's so good to meet you. I don't get to meet many of Vennie's friends.

VENNIE. That's because I never had any. *(Noticing MaDear and Lola.)* Aren't you two a pretty picture? Mother must have you two under gag order again. Mother, you didn't tell me MaDear was in a wheelchair. *(MaDear and Lola stare intently in Vennie's face. They look almost frightened of her, particularly at the earring piercings in her nose and eyebrow.)*

MAYDEE. *(Overlapping.)* Well, that's because it just happened today.

VENNIE. Any minute now y'all can start acting like you're glad to see me. I drove for two days to be a part of this celebration. *(No response from Lola or MaDear.)* Okay, I know how to make you talk. *(Vennie removes her headwrap and she's completely bald. Stunned silence in the room. Lola finds her voice first.)*

LOLA. *(Overlapping.)* Good God! Shaka-Zulu's come to town!

MAYDEE. Vennie, now that's going entirely too far. It's not becoming at all.

LOLA. *(Overlapping.)* All you need is a bone through your nose. Vennie, where in the Sam hell is your hair? Here, put this wig on your damn head! *(She takes off her wig and extends it to Vennie.)*

MADEAR. *(Overlapping.)* And how dem earrangs hang in yo face like dat chile?

VENNIE. *(Laughing.)* Raisa, come on over. If you gon' spend the weekend with them, you might as well get your judgment out the way. *(Raisa walks over. Behind her back, MayDee makes wild gestures for MaDear and Lola to behave.)*

RAISA. I'm Raisa.

MADEAR and LOLA. *(Staring at Raisa's chest.)* Good God Almighty!

VENNIE. This is my grandmother Lola Bird and my great-grandmother Viola Dawkins.

RAISA. It's a pleasure to meet you. *(MaDear and Lola are dumbfounded, fixated on Raisa's chest.)* I can't believe you're Vennie's grandmother. You look so young. My grandmother is five years

31

younger than you, but she likes to say her face looks like the U.S. road map, you know, blue veins and all. *(Laughs loudly, no one else laughs.)*

MAYDEE. Did you hear what Raisa said, Mama? You look so young.

RAISA. *(To MaDear.)* And I can't believe you're ninety today. It's an honor to meet you, Mrs. Dawkins. *(Pause.)* Would you like me to take off my shirt so you might have a better look?

MAYDEE. Oh I don't think that's necessary ...

RAISA. No, it's okay. It's part of my therapy. You know accepting myself ...

MAYDEE. *(Overlapping.)* Vennie, why don't you show Raisa your room? I'm sure you're tired. Maybe you want to freshen up a bit.

VENNIE. *(Doing a scale on the piano.)* We're fresh ... very, very fresh. *(She begins dramatically playing and singing at the top of her lungs, purposely off-key.)* " ... Give me a home ... "

RAISA. *(Overlapping.)* I really don't have any trouble talking about it.

MAYDEE. Vennie would you hush that noise, get off that piano and take Raisa ...

RAISA. *(Overlapping.)* No, it's really okay. *(MayDee crosses to Vennie, closes the piano lid.)*

VENNIE. Mother, it appears that you're a bit stressed. Or is it that you still aren't fond of my singing. *(MayDee shoots Vennie a look to kill. Vennie feigns innocence.)*

RAISA. *(Overlapping.)* Really, I don't mind talking about it. I think it's good to talk about it ... silence equals shame and I have nothing to be ashamed of. So if you have any questions, just ask ...

MAYDEE. *(Overlapping.)* Why don't you take...?

RAISA. *(Overlapping.)* My hair is finally starting to grow back ... and Vennie, she's such a sweetheart, she shaved hers off so I wouldn't feel so alone ...

VENNIE. But then I decided I liked my bald head ... it gave me character, don't you think so Mother?

MAYDEE. Not quite. *(Overlapping.)* You must need your breast ... rest ... *(Mortified at her mistake.)* Vennie, why don't you show Raisa where your room is.

RAISA. *(Overlapping.)* For a long time my mother couldn't say

32

cancer without whispering the word. So you know what I did ... every time I entered the room, I'd yell *(Demonstrates.)* CANCER! as loud as I could. *(Laughs at the memory.)* Cancer! Cancer! Cancer! See it's just a word ...

VENNIE.   Hey MaLola, what you cook? *(Scrounging in the kitchen for food.)* I'm starving ... I hope you make me some cole slaw and some of your chicken ... What else we got to eat?

MAYDEE.   Vennie, your room.

VENNIE.   *(Overlapping.)* We just got here. So why am I getting relegated to the room already? This is a party, isn't it? I brought a whole bunch of music with me. MaLola I got you some old Motown ... come on, I told Raisa this was a good-time house, didn't I? *(Dancing.)* Come on MaLola, what's up? P-A-R-T-Y. *(Sings to MaDear.)* "Happy birthday, you sho' look good to me. I need your loving like a blind man needs to see ... "

MAYDEE.   *(Picking up their bags.)* I'll just take these things to your room.

VENNIE.   Hey, you don't have to tell me twice. I know the drill. Come on, Raisa.

RAISA.   Oh, I'm sorry. I hope I haven't embarrassed anybody. I do tend to have a motor mouth sometimes.

VENNIE.   *(To MaDear and Lola.)* You all better start talking, may not see me for a while.

MAYDEE.   What's that supposed to mean?

RAISA.   We have surprises for all of you.

MAYDEE.   Oh, how nice. Thank you.

VENNIE.   If y'all don't stop staring and start talking, you ain't getting nuttin' from me.

MAYDEE.   Anything, dear.

VENNIE.   Nuttin', honey.

MAYDEE.   Baby, that's a double negative.

VENNIE.   I know that. I majored in English, remember?

MAYDEE.   I'd forgotten. And since your grammar doesn't serve as a reminder ...

VENNIE.   Well, I'm sure you'll get me in shape, Mother, before the day's over.

RAISA.   It was nice meeting you ... all of you. *(Pulls Vennie away.)*

MAYDEE.   *(To Raisa.)* We're glad to have you. *(Handing Vennie*

33

the gift book and bow.) Why don't you take this in the back with you? I appreciate the thought but perhaps next time you can remove the "reduced" sticker.

VENNIE. *(Taking the book, smiling.)* As usual, Mother, it's so good to be home. *(Vennie and Raisa exit.)*

MAYDEE. *(Watches Raisa and Vennie exit, then.)* I've never been so embarrassed. You two were staring at her like she was a damn alien.

LOLA. *(Finding her voice again.)* MayDee, that gal ain't got but one tit!

MAYDEE. So!

LOLA. So? She ain't wearing nuttin'. Did you see she only had one tit?

MADEAR. And dat one tittie bigga den two of mine put together!

LOLA. I see now, I've lived way too long. In all my days, I ain't never seen nuttin' like it. And how are white folks raising they kids? Did you hear she yells cancer at her mother, just like some banshee ... Good God, Lord help me this day ...

MAYDEE. I actually think she has quite a healthy attitude about it. I understand that to some, aesthetically, it might not be that pleasing to the eye ...

LOLA. Aesthetically? And let's not mention the eye. Did you see where Vennie pierced her eye?

MAYDEE. How could one miss it?

LOLA. Look, I'm one for being African but there are limits ... But let's leave Vennie for a minute and go back to what's-her-name ...

MAYDEE. Raisa.

LOLA. Whatever her name is ...

MADEAR. Raisin ...

LOLA. Yeah, that's it. Now that's beyond limits. I wish I could figure out what lesson God's tryin' to teach me this day. They say if you hate something, it's gon' end up in your family. *(Heavenward.)* Okay, Father, I accept your justice but please don't ask me to make sense of it.

MAYDEE. Mama, you might find it offensive, but politically she has a point.

LOLA. Oh MayDee, now don't talk silly. This ain't got nuttin' to do with no politics! Shoot! Politics is Jessie, Martin, the late

34

Harold Washington, bless they souls ... now they was politics. Politics ain't about being the walking wounded.

MAYDEE. It is politics. Her breast is gone, so why should society mandate that she purchase something artificial so we're not offended by the ...

LOLA. She ain't got to purchase something artificial. I'll cut her a kitchen sponge and stick it up there. Put her on a brassiere and you wouldn't know the difference ...

MADEAR. But it ain't no sense wearin a harness if you ain't got nuttin to hitch ...

LOLA. Mama, me and MayDee the ones discussing this. Where's my drink? Where's my damn drink? I can't even get a good drunk on here. And open the window, I'm having one of my flashes.

MAYDEE. What if it were an arm or a leg...?

LOLA. That's different. You can't help that ...

MAYDEE. *(Takes a beat to take in Lola's lack of logic, then.)* Mama, I know it's hard for you to put yourself in somebody else's place, but what if ... what if it were you who had lost a breast?

LOLA. Look, I'm as Christian as the next person, but when something bad happen to you, you ain't supposed to walk around displaying it for the whole world to see. Lord knows I've seen my share of the knife, but you don't see me walking around naked showing everybody ... Now how I look, *(Mocking gestures like she's shaking someone's hand.)* nice to meet you. My name is Lola Bird and I have no shame. *(Lifts up her skirt and parades around and repeats.)* Nice to meet you, my name is Lola Bird. And I'm in therapy.

MADEAR. Now dat ain't a pretty sight. Sit yo tail down gal.

MAYDEE. Mama put your dress down. And please hush before she hears you.

LOLA. It's highway robbery. That's why white folks so crazy now ...

MADEAR. Dey always been crazy ... every last one of 'em.

LOLA. Going to therapy, telling some stranger all they business. AND PAY HIM GOOD MONEY! Pay him good money to tell 'em to introduce theirselves by taking they shirts off. Therapy my behind ... I'm sorry MayDee, but if Vennie gon' be that way she could have least gotten herself a nice black girl with two breasts, now I could deal with that! And offering to show us. Did you hear her offer to take her shirt off? She was gon' show us.

35

MADEAR. Yeah. I was waitin!

LOLA. Now don't that beat all. Mama's done gon' freaky too. MayDee, it must be this house. *(Starts searching the floor of the house.)* Something is seeping through the pores of this house. I declare it is. My horoscope told me to beware of cosmic forces today …

MADEAR. *(Loud.)* SISTER, SISTER, COME HERE.

LOLA. What is it now Mama?

MADEAR. WHEW, FETCH ME A TOWEL. MY BREASTS DONE FILLED UP WID MILK! OOOHHH!! *(Cupping her breast, opens her dress, takes part of the shawl and stuffs it by her breast, presumably to catch the milk.)*

LOLA. Mama, don't start that. I done had enough shocks on this day.

MAYDEE. *(Overlapping.)* You smell something? Oh shit. I forgot the rolls in the oven. *(Races over to the oven, removes the rolls that are burned.)* Burned.

MADEAR. *(Still holding her breasts.)* Man, dis gon' be some kinda birthday. Burnt food, Vennie done gone bald and got a white gal wid one tittie and you an me gon' have us a baby. Milk flowin just like de Mississippi. Whew … *(Lights. Music, a song like The Shirelles' "Mama Said."*)*

* See Special Note on Songs and Recordings on copyright page.

ACT TWO

Scene 1

At lights, we see Vennie in the mirror. She slowly strips away some of her rings from her various piercings. With each removal she appears to disarm herself, becoming more and more vulnerable looking. She finally wraps her head. We leave Vennie and find MaDear outside under the tree and, as usual, she's having a conversation with herself. Raisa appears whistling.

RAISA. *(Entering.)* There you are. Where's everybody?

MADEAR. In the shed out back.

RAISA. I'm Raisa, again.

MADEAR. Pleased to make yo acquaintance Miss Raisin.

RAISA. Would you like your surprise now? *(Opens the bag, pulls out oversized T-shirts.)* Let's see, now which one is yours? I did the screens myself. I'm an artist. At least I'm trying to be one. Yeah, here it is. This one's for you. *(She holds a shirt that reads "Ninety and Still Kicking.")* Do you like it?

MADEAR. I bet you wish you'd died.

RAISA. *(Taken aback for a moment, pause.)* Yes. There were moments I thought I had.

MADEAR. Dey want me to b'lieve Man is dead.

RAISA. Your husband?

MADEAR. He lef me. He lef me here all by myself. Who gon' take care of dis baby? De only reason I stay wid him is dese chil'ren. He got other women in dat shed out back. I sees 'em ... drankin' an' doin' the devil's dance ... he dance wid 'em ... ain't never danced wid me, just jumps on top of me ... Man, you hurt me ... you hurt me.

37

RAISA. I'm sorry. I'm so sorry.

MADEAR. I gits so cold here.

RAISA. Well, why don't I take you inside and get you warmed up? *(She wheels MaDear inside the house, then drapes a shawl around MaDear's shoulders.)*

RAISA. Is that better? *(MaDear nods yes.)* How 'bout a foot rub? That's always good to warm a body. *(She begins massaging MaDear's feet. MaDear lets her, studying her closely. Finally.)*

MADEAR. You got you a bad wound?

RAISA. You wanna see? *(MaDear nods yes. Raisa kneels, slowly opens her shirt as she talks.)* I'm warning you, it's not very pretty. *(Reveals the scar.)*

MADEAR. Oh my. *(Taken aback by the scar, but then tenderly touches it.)*

RAISA. I never thought I'd miss anything so much. As you can see, I've never been a real beauty but what me and Cover Girl couldn't cover, this body used to. It used to get me some attention but now I'm operating at a real cosmetic handicap, don't you think?

MADEAR. *(MaDear shakes her head no.)* Chile, you ain't got nuttin' to be 'shamed of. Some folks wear dey scars on de inside ... you jus wearin' yours on de outside.

RAISA. I guess. *(Getting up and buttoning her shirt.)*

MADEAR. I'm tellin' you dat scar ain't nuttin' to be 'shamed of. A scar ain't nuttin' but a witness. It's yo history. Just like dis belly. *(MaDear unsnaps her dress, shows Raisa her profuse stretch marks.)* All my babies lef dey mark ... Go 'head touch 'em, dey ain't gon' bite you. *(Raisa touches her belly.)* You show me a woman dat ain't gotta scar somewhere an I'll show you a woman dat ain't lived nuttin' but a lie. It's dem inside scars, dem de ones you gotta watch out for. Dey'll tear you up tryin to git loose. I know. But yours, it's breathin' good ... yes sir ... breathin' real good. *(Raisa smiles, pleased.)* Chile, you got chil'ren?

RAISA. A son.

MADEAR. A son? And he yo pride an joy, ain't he?

RAISA. Un-hun. We wanted another child, a girl, but after I got sick ...

MADEAR. Ain't never wanted no fast gal 'round up in my house.

Ain't no house big enough for two women. You must not been married long ...

RAISA. Almost six years.

MADEAR. Today's my anniver'sry. Seventy years today. Blessed wid one son, he comin' for me today ... Un-hun. You got somebody comin' for you?

RAISA. No. My husband and I are separated.

MADEAR. Say what?

RAISA. He had a hard time ... you know, adjusting ... *(Gestures to her missing breast.)*

MADEAR. Ain't dat 'bout nuttin'? Dey took yo tittie an he too fool he gon' let de tittie take him 'long wid it. I wouldn't have another man if he sprouted wings and flew.

RAISA. It's really not his fault. It's bad enough trying to make ends meet, raise a child. He's in law school. I was trying to start my own word processing business, you know something I could do at home so I could spend more time with my son ... but then I up and got sick ...

MADEAR. De marriage vow say through sickness and in health.

RAISA. I know. But a vow only tells you what to do. It doesn't really tell you how. We got married so young ...

MADEAR. Well marriage ain't sumptin' you wanna do when you old enough to know better ...

RAISA. He kept buying me nightgowns ...

MADEAR. Man ain't never bought nuttin' for me to wear ... he jus buy for Lola, always Lola.

RAISA. Well, you can bet Mark didn't buy the gowns for me ... I never slept in a gown the whole time we were married ... I really miss my son ... but you understand why I had to leave, don't you?

MADEAR. I ain't never been able to leave nowhere even when I was pas' ready to go ...

RAISA. Me neither. But I knew I couldn't keep living with someone who had no clue about what I was going through. My husband kept saying your body's changed, honey, but you haven't. Isn't that the stupidest thing you ever heard? It was like he was waiting on me to teach him all over again how to love me, how to even touch me ... and who has time to teach school when the clock's ticking. I don't even know this body anymore so how in the world am I going

39

to teach him?

MADEAR. *(Suddenly.)* When you look at me and my body, do you see ugly Miss Raisin?

RAISA. Oh no, Mrs. Dawkins. You are so beautiful. *(lovingly running her hand across MaDear's cheek.)* I'd kill to have soft skin like yours. Since all the treatments, it seems like my skin never has a drop of moisture.

MADEAR. She keep saying I'm ugly.

RAISA. Who? Who says that?

MADEAR. Momo. She waitin' on me. I sees her every time I look in de mirror. She say you's one ugly child of a dog Viola and she laugh and laugh at me. "You so nappy-headed ... how I birth'd sumptin' so coon black ugly ... " She gon' whip me, Miss Raisin. I know she gon' whip me till I bleeds. She say I'm so ugly.

RAISA. Well, she's wrong, Mrs. Dawkins. She's wrong.

MADEAR. That's what Man say ... he married me prove her wrong ... *(Looking around for the nonexistent garden.)* He'll be comin' in from de fields wantin' his dinner ... and I ain't got nuttin' cooked. You see my veg'ebles, dey just keep dying on me. Got cows to milk but dey won't come when I call ... my chickens need seein' after ... did you see 'em 'round here?

RAISA. Maybe I should get ...

MADEAR. No, I gots to git home ... and my daughter, she done lef me ... she and Man, dey just left me ... dey always leavin' me behind ... *(Very confused.)* and I gits so cold since dey been gone ... I don't wanna die here, Miss Raisin ... I can hear it comin' ... Don't you hear it?

RAISA. Mrs. Dawkins ...

MADEAR. *(Grabbing Raisa's hand.)* I cain't jus sit here and let it git me. I know you hears it Miss Raisin ... don't let it git you. You hear it?

RAISA. I hear it Mrs. Dawkins but you know how I keep it at bay? Everyday I go to Europe, in my mind. I'm buying me some mean Italian shoes and I'm sitting in one of those little cafes all day philosophizing, smoking cigarettes, drinking exotic coffees and wines. You wanna hear today's trip? *(MaDear nods yes.)* Okay, I'm sitting outside a little cafe and I'm wearing a black beret, kind of cocked to the side with a big diamond butterfly pen right in the middle. I used to dream in zirconia, but these days this girl's dreaming in diamonds. Anyway, I got this huge diamond right smack in the middle of my beret. I'm a beacon of rainbow color. You picturing me now, aren't you? *(MaDear nods agreeably, excitedly.)* Okay, so I got this brilliant light radiating off my forehead. It's just about blinding to anybody who comes within a hundred feet. So of course everybody has to stop and ask, where'd you'd get such a magnificent pin? And I laugh oh so haughtily … *(Demonstrates her auteur laugh and accent.)* "Oh this ol' thing … well darlings, it's just my latest creation." And they're speechless, utterly, utterly entranced with me as they move closer, *(MaDear moves closer.)* their eyes scanning my body, up and down, left to right, head to toe and they're transformed. Yes, you can see it on their faces. Did I happen to mention except for the body paint, I'm stark naked while all this is going on? *(Raisa laughs; MaDear laughs too, claps with joy.)* Oh yes, and then the clapping starts. It's feverish with excitement. *(Clapping her hands to demonstrate.)* Magnifico! Magnifico! I think that's how you say it but anyway, they're throwing flowers at my feet. It's unanimous. They have declared me a work of art. Raisa Krementz's body is a work of art! *(Touches the place of her missing breast.)* Even here. *(Beat.)* God, I wanna go. I really, really wanna go. I can almost taste it. Even it's only for a day. *(Beat.)* They found a new spot on my liver. The doctors said it's chemo time, but I said no, it's Raisa's time and Raisa's not in the mood to share a second of it with chemo … not now. I just want to get away, to have a piece of my dream before it's too late.

MADEAR. *(Suddenly.)* Will you take me home wid you? I cleans good. I'll do wash an tend yo chil'ren, and I won't git in de way of yo business … you can count on Viola … won't be no trouble … no trouble at all. I'm beggin you Miss Raisin, I just wanna see my home again.

RAISA. I know. Why don't I help you put on your new shirt? Watch your head. *(She gently puts the shirt over MaDear's head, fixes it on her.)* There. Don't you look nice. Ninety and still kicking. You must stay true to your shirt, I say you gotta go out kicking. Come on, let me see how high you can kick …

MADEAR. Gal, I cain't kick. My legs are weighted down …

RAISA. I bet you can kick. *(She kneels down and stars lifting*

41

MaDear's feet and leg.) See, you still have some kick left in you. Come on, aim for the old kisser here. Let's see how much kick either one of us has. Ooh, and the left jaw takes a dive … Ooh, and there goes the right … *(With Raisa's assistance MaDear starts kicking toward Raisa's face, both are clearly enjoying themselves. Vennie enters, watches Raisa and MaDear for a minute.)* You got me on the ropes. And she's down *(Raisa falls down, counts.)* … 1-2 …

VENNIE. *(To Raisa.)* I'm so glad you're feeling better. *(Joins them.)* If you could see how you two look.

MADEAR. *(Suddenly and viciously hits at Vennie.)* Git away from here, split-tail. We's playin' dis game. *(Vennie backs off obviously hurt. MaDear starts laughing, gestures for Raisa to resume playing with her feet. Just then Lola and MayDee enter carrying chips and dip.)*

LOLA. What in the sam hell? Mama, put your legs down!

RAISA. I'm sorry, we were just playing. *(Exhausted, looks to Vennie to help her up, which Vennie does.)*

LOLA. I leave the room for one minute and y'all start using my mama for entertainment.

MAYDEE. *(To Raisa.)* You've worked a miracle because I can't remember the last time I saw MaDear laugh out loud.

LOLA. What you mean? Mama and me, we laugh every day while you at school, don't we, Mama? You just keep me in stitches. *(False exaggerated laugh.)* Hee, hee, hee. I thought I was getting a hernia one day I laughed so hard …

MAYDEE. Vennie, is something wrong?

VENNIE. No. Why does something always have to be wrong?

MAYDEE. I just asked you a simple question …

VENNIE. I was just standing here. Why do you always automatically assume…?

LOLA. I'm so happy my little Pick-Me-Up is home. Pour MaLola a drink, baby. A little CC and wet it with soda and a little lime slice.

VENNIE. Coming right up. Raisa?

RAISA. Nothing for me.

VENNIE. What about for MaDear?

LOLA. Nothing for her.

VENNIE. Okay, MaLola, just you and me living dangerously.

MAYDEE. Well, did it occur to you that I might care for something?

VENNIE. Oh. What?

42

MAYDEE. Thank you but I'll get it myself.

VENNIE. I said I'd get it.

MAYDEE. Don't do me any big favors. *(Crosses and pours herself a little wine.)*

MADEAR. Pour me a taste outta dat brown jar. Dat's my medicine.

LOLA. Mama, now you know that ain't your medicine, that's liquor. ALCOHOL!

MADEAR. Don't tell me 'bout what I know.

MAYDEE. It's her birthday. A little taste wouldn't hurt.

LOLA. Okay, but don't look at me when she starts talking silly.

RAISA. We forgot to give them their shirts. Do you like it, Mrs. Dawkins?

MAYDEE. It's very nice. Do you like it MaDear?

MADEAR. I'm kickin'.

VENNIE. Raisa did the screens. I did the slogans. *(To MayDee.)* This one's for you.

MAYDEE. Thank you. *(Reading it.)* "Tenure by Popular Demand." That's catchy ...

VENNIE. Put it on ...

MAYDEE. Oh no, not till I hear something.

VENNIE. You'll get it. You never fail.

MAYDEE. *(Pointedly.)* I try not to.

LOLA. Where's mine?

VENNIE. Right here. *(Hands it to Lola. Lola reads it silently, folds it up and places it to the side.)* Don't you like it?

LOLA. Yes baby. MaLola likes everything you do. It's very nice.

VENNIE. You didn't show anybody.

MAYDEE. Let's see it, Mama.

LOLA. Later.

RAISA. Maybe you would've liked another color ...

VENNIE. *(Picking up the shirt, showing everyone, reading.)* "The best damn Grandmother."

MAYDEE. *(Laughing.)* I can see why she didn't want to show it.

VENNIE. I thought you'd love this.

LOLA. I said it was nice. I just don't know when I'll have occasion to wear it.

VENNIE. Tonight. These are our party T-shirts. MaDear, you gon' wear your shirt?

MADEAR. Couldn't beat it off me. A little more outta my jug dere baby.

LOLA. Mama, you don't need anything else to drink ...

MAYDEE. Sure we'll put them on, won't we Mama?

LOLA. Speak for yourself.

MAYDEE. *(Crossing to the phone.)* Well, I guess I'll just unplug this here telephone for the rest of the day ...

LOLA. *(Grabbing the shirt.)* Just what I always wanted. I'm a tie mine up here on the side.

VENNIE. I have another surprise in the car.

MAYDEE. *(A little expectantly.)* Oh?

VENNIE. It's for MaDear. *(Vennie exits, there's a long silence, much clearing of the throat as they all decide what to talk about.)*

LOLA. So ...

RAISA. I'm really enjoying myself.

LOLA. Don't take much to amuse you, do it?

MAYDEE. Mama.

LOLA. So how long you known our little Vennie?

RAISA. Oh for a while now, but after I left my husband ...

LOLA. You got a husband?

MAYDEE. I hope you like chicken Raisa ...

RAISA. *(Overlapping.)* Yes ... And a five-year-old son ...

MAYDEE. I think it's baked? Is it baked chicken Mama?

LOLA. *(Not taking her focus from Raisa.)* I don't know MayDee! So, your husband know you and Vennie friends?

MAYDEE. Did you say Raisa that you're a native Floridian?

RAISA. In a way. We moved there from Wisconsin when I was twelve. My father always wanted to retire there ... my parents had me late ...

LOLA. *(Overlapping.)* And does he have a little friend too?

MAYDEE. *(Overlapping.)* You say your parents are retired?

RAISA. *(Having difficulty keeping up with the order of questions being fired off.)* Yes. No. I mean who exactly are we talking about?

LOLA. Your husband.

MAYDEE. *(Overlapping.)* Your parents. Did Vennie tell you the two of us took a drive across country once?

LOLA. *(Impatiently.)* MayDee, why don't you ever let me talk sometimes?

MAYDEE. *(As if Lola hadn't spoken.)* I was working on my master's thesis I believe. She was bored out of her mind. But you know how teenagers are, except Vennie always had the attention span of a rock.

LOLA. Yoo-hoo ... Yoo-hoo ... I really wish I could get a word in edgewise, Miss Diarrhea of the Mouth ...

RAISA. Oh, I'm sorry. What did you ask me again?

LOLA. I just wanted to know honey has your husband had occasion to make Vennie's acquaintance?

RAISA. Yes, he's met her ...

LOLA. I see. *(A pointed look thrown MayDee's way.)* Now we getting somewhere.

MAYDEE. Mama ...

LOLA. Same time you met her?

RAISA. Oh no. I met Vennie at a bar. Actually a woman's bar. I had never been to one so I thought what the hell ... let's go all the way ... *(Lola throws MayDee a look.)* Left my bra and the prosthesis on the front seat of the car. I was scared out of my wits but the closer I got to the front door the lighter I felt.

LOLA. *(Another pointed look to MayDee.)* That so?

RAISA. Yeah. Vennie was on stage and I was blown away. She can really sing. When she smiled at me I knew right then and there I had found a friend. We bought a pitcher of margaritas and let me tell you I got so giddy ... You ever been scared and excited all at once...?

LOLA. Yes, men do that to me.

RAISA. Well, Vennie did it for me that night. She brought me on stage and I started singing and I can't even carry a tune ... but there I was wailing my heart out, drunk as a skunk, and Vennie worked that crowd until they gave me a standing ovation ... can you imagine? Me. It was wild ... I'm telling you things I would never imagine doing, Vennie's talked me into ...

LOLA. Is that so. And what else has she talked you into?

RAISA. *(Takes a moment.)* I guess you can say she's talked me back into life. Vennie has this way of making you feel like you can do anything, no matter how wild and crazy ... she doesn't have a lot of expectations ... she just rolls with whatever comes her way ... *(Vennie enters.)*

VENNIE. *(Enters.)* Did I miss something?

RAISA. No, I was just boring them with how we met.

LOLA. Yeah, it was some story …

VENNIE. MaDear, I started these so you could have a little garden. I remember when I used to come to visit and you let me work in the garden. You remember?

MADEAR. You ain't never wanted to work in de garden. All you knew to do was turn up yo tail … And he was mine. He was mine, split-tail.

LOLA. Mama, that's Vennie. You stop being ugly now.

VENNIE. *(Clearly hurt.)* Doesn't she know me?

LOLA. Of course she know you. She just putting on.

VENNIE. MaDear, I got peppers and onions, tomato plants … and sunflowers … And I thought we could plant them together. We even stopped in Mississippi on our way through and I got you some dirt. *(With the mention of dirt, MayDee immediately at attention.)*

RAISA. Yeah, I didn't know what she was doing. I came out of the filling station and there she was on the ground digging up dirt.

MAYDEE. Does that bag have a hole in it?

VENNIE. No, mother. Relax. I'm not making a mess …

MADEAR. *(Lovingly fingering the plants.)* Dey don't allow me no garden here. Back home I gots me a big garden … Everythang planted I planted. I planted dem wid dese here hands … Man, show 'em my garden … show 'em Man …

LOLA. Mama, we got company now, so no need for you to talk foolish … What your friend Raisa gon' think … you talking out your head like that…?

RAISA. I understand … My grandmother went through the same thing … she talked to people that weren't there all the time. I just figured she had a direct line to the angels.

LOLA. *(Not sure how to follow up.)* Well, we don't like to encourage her. We'd like to be the only angels she talks to.

MAYDEE. I really wish you would've consulted me first about this garden. It was a nice thought but …

VENNIE. What's there to consult? The yard is huge.

MAYDEE. And costly to keep up. Mama, you still going to do my hair?

LOLA. Yeah, get a towel. *(MayDee exits.)*

VENNIE. I wasn't intending on planting a farm.

MAYDEE. *(Off.)* That's not the point.

VENNIE. What's the point then?

LOLA. The point is a garden needs a lot of attention. It's a lot of work.

VENNIE. Grandma, I know that.

LOLA. What you call me?

VENNIE. MaLola.

LOLA. That's better. I don't know what's gotten into you. Grandma! The idea!

MAYDEE. *(Overlapping, off.)* Vennie, no one has time to take care of a garden ...

VENNIE. MaDear doesn't ask for much. If she can't be in Mississippi at least you all can do is try and create it for her here.

LOLA. Create Mississippi?!

MAYDEE. *(Entering with towel and hair oil, comb and brush.)* I'm not sure I want Mississippi in Park Forest, Illinois ...

LOLA. Well I'm sure. I ain't never wanted it. I didn't care too much for Mississippi when I was in Mississippi, I'm tellin' you the truth.

MADEAR. Dat's yo home gal. I birthed you an' weaned you ...

LOLA. And don't a day go by when you ain't reminding me ...

MAYDEE. *(Overlapping.)* We'll discuss this garden thing later. Until then, Raisa, honey, why don't you do me a favor and set those things by the back door on top of the garbage can. And please be very careful with that dirt.

RAISA. Sure. *(She exchanges looks with Vennie who is silently fuming. Raisa eventually exits out back.)*

MAYDEE. By the way, Vennie, I got you a little something. Of course I didn't know you'd be wearing it with a bald *head (Goes to the closet, retrieves the outfit with much flourish.)*, but anyway Saks was having a magnificent sale ...

VENNIE. *(Looks at the outfit, Lola starts to look upwards, whistles as she waits on the fireworks.)* You got to be kidding. I'm not wearing that sh ...

LOLA. Vennie, watch that mouth. *(To MayDee, hardly able to contain her laughter.)* I told you.

VENNIE. You could've at least taken the tags off but then again the rules are different for you, right?

47

LOLA. I thought you ...

MAYDEE. I wasn't sure if it would fit ... *(Raisa enters.)*

VENNIE. Mother, that ain't happening. Maybe you should wear it or get your money back.

LOLA. *(Noticing how hurt MayDee looks.)* Well, let's see. I think with the right kind of jewelry ... *(Takes off her necklace, puts it up next to the outfit.)* Get some big earrings and a pretty silk scarf ... then ...

VENNIE. Have to accessorize it beyond recognition ...

LOLA and VENNIE. Accessorize it to death. *(They both laugh.)*

MAYDEE. I'm glad I can be a source of humor for you two ...

RAISA. I like it. I think it's classy.

VENNIE. Then why don't you wear it. *(Raisa gives Vennie a pointed look.)* Okay Mother, thank you. Thank you so much. It's a nice outfit. I mean it's perfect for church or dinner with the Pope. Just kidding.

MAYDEE. I didn't mean it for everyday wear. I thought we could go shopping and maybe get some matching pumps ...

LOLA. Come on, if you want me to do your hair ... Vennie, did you put some liquor in this drink?

VENNIE. Yeah. Ain't enough poison? Want it stronger?

MAYDEE. *(Still talking about the suit.)* Why don't you put it with your things.

LOLA. *(Overlapping.)* A drink ain't never strong enough over here. I can come here tipping over drunk and sober up soon's I step over the threshold.

MAYDEE. Vennie, I asked you...?

VENNIE. MaLola, I got a bottle in the car. You wanna try that?

MAYDEE. Vennie, I was talking ...

LOLA. *(Overlapping.)* Thank you kindly ma'am, but Lola don't drink cheap liquor ...

VENNIE. *(Laughing.)* Now you didn't have to go there ...

MAYDEE. Vennie, did you hear me?

VENNIE. *(Impatiently.)* What?

MAYDEE. I said take the suit and put it with your other things.

VENNIE. Why don't you just hang it back in the closet, Mother? *(To Lola as she takes her glass to add more booze.)* Let me try this thing again.

MAYDEE. *(Attempting to hide her annoyance for Raisa's benefit.)* Oh. Okay. Fine.

LOLA. Put it way back in the closet. *(Vennie and Lola burst into laughter. Raisa looks embarrassed for MayDee.)*

RAISA. If you want, I'll put it with our stuff. *(She takes the outfit from MayDee who offers a grateful smile. Raisa exits with the outfit through the hall.)*

MAYDEE. By the way, did you get that other package I sent you a few weeks back?

VENNIE. Which one? You send me one every other week.

MAYDEE. Would it be too much to ask for you to call or send a note...?

VENNIE. You never give me a chance. You send me something and you call me the same day you mailed it to ask me if I received it. *(On Raisa's entrance.)* Doesn't she Raisa? *(Raisa doesn't respond. MayDee sits and Lola starts oiling and scratching her scalp.)*

MAYDEE. I can't remember. Did I send you some catalogs, some packets on financial aid?

VENNIE. Did you send me something on financial aid? Mother, you been sending me ...

LOLA. Now who's bringing up school? *(To Vennie.)* And I want you to know young lady I'm still mad that I didn't get to go to that graduation. Bought me a new dress and everything. Had my tears stored up and they was front row tears. Next thing I know your Mama telling me you decided not to go through the ceremony ... now that hurt me ...

RAISA. *(Suddenly interceding.)* Can I get anyone anything? *(Lola and Vennie gesture no in their own specific way.)*

MAYDEE. *(Smiles warmly at Raisa.)* No, I'm fine. But thank you so much for asking. *(Offers a pointed look in Vennie's direction, a look that reads that Vennie could take a few pointers from Raisa.)*

VENNIE. *(Teasing Lola.)* Look who's poutin', your lip all poked out ... you know you can't stay mad ... Come on, MaLola, smile at your little Pick-Me-Up ...

LOLA. *(Playfully hitting at Vennie.)* Vennie, go on, get outta my face.

MAYDEE. *(Overlapping.)* Don't you think she would be a great teacher, Mama? *(Raisa and Vennie start decorating the room with party streamers.)*

49

VENNIE. Hmnn, maybe it is my grammar ... maybe I am speaking another language. You just don't seem to understand me when I say I don't wanna teach.

MADEAR. *(Reenacting an imaginary classroom.)* Good mornin' Mrs. Dawkins. Mornin chil'ren. Dis is our lesson for today ...

MAYDEE. *(Overlapping, trying to ignore MaDear.)* You don't have to teach. Just have it, something to fall back on.

VENNIE. If I have something to fall back on, then I'll never learn to stand up.

MAYDEE. See? See what I mean? That was quite a profound statement dear. And that's what I'm saying, you have a good mind, a splendid mind, doesn't she Mama?

LOLA. I don't get in between you all's business. *(Oiling MayDee's scalp.)*

VENNIE. Why do we get into this every time I come home?

MAYDEE. *(Sarcastic.)* Every time? What? Once every two years, you manage to make an appearance? And of course it's usually because you want something. Of course this time you may surprise me ...

LOLA. She'd come home more if you'd stop nagging her about going back to school, not everyone love school like you do. I couldn't stand it myself.

VENNIE. I heard that!

MAYDEE. Mama, I was speaking with Vennie.

LOLA. Well s'cuse the hell out of me, I ain't gotta say shit more today.

VENNIE. Look Mother, here's the deal. I'm going to sing. That's what I wanna do, that's what I'm gonna do ... By hook or by crook ...

LOLA. Then sing in the shower. Sing in church. You could come go with me on Sunday. Plenty opportunities to sing, but you gotta eat, gotta have a place to live ...

MADEAR. I sing for de Lord. *(Starts singing.)* "I'm on de battle field for my Lord, yes I'm on de battlefield ... "

LOLA. Mama, please. *(Crosses to MaDear, opens the Bible and firmly puts it in her lap.)* We can sing later. Here.

MAYDEE. If you're so bent on this music career, then take some classes. Train yourself properly. Perhaps you could move back home ...

VENNIE. You don't really want that now, do you, Mother?

MAYDEE. Just until you get on your feet.

VENNIE. Hm, all this time I thought you preferred me on my knees ...

MAYDEE. The university has a fine program ... I'm sure we can stay out of each other's way ...

VENNIE. Mother, the tape is stuck. Why don't we turn it over?

RAISA. Mrs. Lakeland, have you heard Vennie sing?

LOLA. Of course ...

MAYDEE. Yes, I've seen her, several times.

VENNIE. I've improved since high school.

MAYDEE. *(Barely masking the sarcasm.)* Oh have you?

RAISA. She has this energy, this amazing ability to work an audience, especially when's she's singing her own songs. She writes the most beautiful songs. The crowds just love her.

LOLA. Crowds don't last and they'll make sure you don't either.

RAISA. But she's so good. She dances ...

LOLA. Well now she gets that from me 'cause her mother got two left feet that wouldn't know right if she pointed them there. But now ain't nobody can beat her on that piano. MayDee used to could make that piano sing, could bring tears to your eyes.

MAYDEE. A long time ago, but we were talking about Vennie.

LOLA. Scrape and scratch ... scrimping so she could keep up with her lessons ...

MAYDEE. And I thank you for that, Mother, but I ...

LOLA. And the more she played white, the harder I had to work ...

MAYDEE. Music is music. It has no color.

LOLA. Yes it does ... green! Them teachers said you were gifted. Even had you convinced black music was trash, but I went along, wanted you to make it.

MAYDEE. I appreciate that, Mother ...

LOLA. Did without so she could keep up with them lessons. One year I didn't even have boots, snow up to my neck but as long as she was happy ...

MAYDEE. I learned early how fickle the entertainment business could be ... If I had been white, maybe things would have been different.

VENNIE. Well, nowadays you don't have to be white to make it.

LOLA. Says who? Now don't talk stupid, Miss College Graduate. White people still control everything, no offense Raisa.

RAISA. Just so you know, I'm Jewish.

LOLA. Well, that's nice, but colored folks, we don't divide white people up like that. Now as I was saying just 'cause white folks control everything you still got to have a little gumption, a little spine.

MAYDEE. Vennie, it's not that I mind you singing ...

VENNIE. Thanks. I'm glad you don't mind me living my own life.

LOLA. *(Brushing MayDee's hair a little too hard.)* One audition, one freakin audition, spent my last dime on you a new outfit and Willie brought her home crying, crying her eyes out ... I thought somebody had beat you silly ...

MAYDEE. I just don't want to see you hurt ...

LOLA. Shoot, life is full of hurts. She broke her hand ... that cost me, and then her hand healed but did she stop the whining? Noooo. She just gave up and in my book, you never give up.

MAYDEE. Sometimes it's not that easy, Mama. *(Using her cigarette lighter, Lola burns the hair from the comb while Raisa stares in confused silence.)*

LOLA. Don't tell me about easy. If you see Easy, send him to me. I'd like to make his acquaintance. Shit. Easy laid out a silk purse for you and left me with the bill.

MAYDEE. *(Old seething anger and bitter pain.)* And what do you think he left me with, Mama? *(European accent.)* "You people have so much rhythm, why don't you play what you know?" But I played what I knew ... Debussy, Bach, the Liszt Sonata, the Chopin Barcarole. That's the music I loved ... but nobody ever cared about what I loved ... nobody protected me. *(Studies her hands, takes a beat to stretch them, then quietly to Vennie.)* And I will never let that happen to you ... I will not see you hurt ...

VENNIE. You can't direct my life ...

LOLA. Vennie, your mother is not gon' be here forever. And Lord knows my days are numbered. We only trying to help. We wouldn't be so bothered if we didn't love you ...

VENNIE. Then stop loving me so much. Just chill.

LOLA. What? Chill? *(Threatens her with the brush.)* I'll chill right on your behind. You ain't too old to hit the floor.

MADEAR. Spare de rod, spoil de child.

MAYDEE. And I can't keep sending you envelopes. You know what I'm talking about, Vennie Lakeland ...

VENNIE. I never asked.

MAYDEE. Nor refused.

LOLA. Talking to me about some damn chill! What kind of shit ...

MAYDEE. Mama please.

VENNIE. You all are embarrassing me.

MAYDEE. Well, I don't mean to ...

LOLA. I'm a do more than embarrass you. Your Mama's telling you the truth. She works hard for her money.

MADEAR. And de truth shall set you free ...

LOLA. That's right Mama.

MAYDEE. I'm concerned. I just want the best for you, baby.

LOLA. We both want the best for you ...

MAYDEE. Mama, would you please let me talk ...

LOLA. Then talk. I ain't stopped you from talking. I barely opened my mouth since Vennie walked through that door. You the one that's going on and on about the past ...

MAYDEE. As I was saying, I don't want to see you playing one night stands the rest of your life ...

LOLA. In women's bars at that ...

VENNIE. I don't just work in women's bars ...

MAYDEE. Making fifty here and twenty-five there ...

VENNIE. I make more than that ...

LOLA. Then look like you'd buy something decent to put on your behind.

MAYDEE. What happens when you get too old to shake your behind? Then what?

VENNIE. Is that all you think I do?

MAYDEE. What I think is that you have not provided yourself with any real safety net.

VENNIE. Safety net?! Who cares about being safe? I happen to like danger.

LOLA. I got danger for you. Say something else about chill.

MAYDEE. But you can do so much more with your life Vennie ... put yourself in a position that you don't have to worry about anything or anybody ...

VENNIE. Not worrying about anybody? Don't you think that's

more your speed, Mother?

MAYDEE. I worry about you all the time, Vennie. What I'm trying to say is I just want you to do better.

VENNIE. But what if I don't want to do better?

LOLA. You oughtta wanna do better by them clothes you wear. A college graduate and still living poor as a church mouse.

MAYDEE. It's not the clothes that I object to. I know the styles change …

LOLA. A raggedy woman will never attract a man!

VENNIE. Who says I want to attract a man?

MAYDEE. Can we stay on the subject?

LOLA. See! What I tell you? You 'member that Johnson gal?

MAYDEE. Mama, please.

VENNIE. What I'd like is for you to let me live my life as I see fit. Poor, raggedy, whatever.

LOLA. And you want to live it without a man, don't you? Don't you?

MAYDEE. She doesn't need a man … what I'm concerned about …

LOLA. See, and you wonder why she's like she is.

VENNIE. Like what? And what is all this talk about men? Nobody in this room is with a man.

LOLA. Speak for yourself …

MADEAR. (Overlapping.) I gots me a man, seventy years … even when I didn't want him, I had me a man.

VENNIE. Well, Mother, hasn't had a man since before I was born.

MAYDEE. Vennie! I don't appreciate you discussing my business …

VENNIE. But it's okay to discuss mine.

LOLA. Now she gotta point there, MayDee …

MAYDEE. Well, let's just discuss the gigolo …

LOLA. Hey, hey now, anybody care for some dip?

VENNIE. If I meet a man I like, then cool, we'll deal. It's not complicated. If I don't it ain't gon' make me crazy.

MAYDEE. (Correcting.) Going to …

VENNIE. What?

MAYDEE. Going to make me crazy, not gon' make …

VENNIE. See, this is why I don't come home.

LOLA. But you call here everyday and collect …

MAYDEE. I find it so astounding that you never fail to make sure everything careens out of control every time you come home.

VENNIE. So this is all my fault?

MAYDEE. Who said anything about fault? Let's just table this. I want MaDear to have a good day. We have plenty of time to discuss this later. How long are you two planning to stay?

VENNIE. You started it.

MAYDEE. Started what? What did I start this time? All I asked you was how long you plan to stay. How is that an invitation for conflict?

VENNIE. Mother please! It's what you start every time I come home ...

MAYDEE. I have not started one thing today ... all I asked ...

VENNIE. You and your little ice pick ... soon's you see me, you go to town. Pick, pick, pick. My clothes ain't right, pick, my hair ain't right, pick, pick, my grammar ain't right ... triple pick ... sum it up, I ain't right ...

MAYDEE. Whine ... whine ... whine ... grow up, Vennie.

VENNIE. I would if you'd let me.

MAYDEE. That's not true.

VENNIE. *(Sarcastically, but delivered calmly with a smile.)* Oh, let's get real. Y'all have performed for the company so let's take it on down to Front Street. See Raisa, I'm something to be bought for, organized and then laid out so others can marvel at how wonderful MayDee Lakeland is ... how she overcame every obstacle to get her three degrees in one hand and raise me single-handedly in the other ... and what's that commercial ... never let 'em see you sweat. Well that's MayDee Lakeland ... you'll never see her sweat, queen of control ... that's what we all love about her ...

RAISA. Vennie, I don't think ...

VENNIE. *(Feigned innocence, as if the thought just occurred to her.)* Um, do we have an itinerary this weekend, Mother? I was telling Raisa that you always made sure I participated in every activity: karate, dance, art, gymnastics. So did the secretary remember to outline Vennie's activities, you know in those fifteen minute increments ... what Mother-dear is going to do with daughter-dear this weekend. *(MayDee quietly disposes of the itinerary.)* Oh come on now, you didn't leave our time together to chance. 'Cause then maybe you would have to enjoy me. And that would be too

55

much like right, wouldn't it Mother? S'pecially given that you don't even like me.

MAYDEE. *(Pause, embarrassed to have this conversation in front of Raisa, MayDee laughs.)* You're just like your grandmother, such a wicked sense of humor. I love you Vennie. All I ever wanted was to protect you. Don't you know how much I love you, whatever you do?

VENNIE. What I know is being your daughter hurts ... bad or should I say badly ...

MAYDEE. You can't mean that. *(Exits with hair stuff.)*

LOLA. Now look what you done. You done gone and hurt your Mama's feelings. I don't know what's wrong with this generation. They wanna blame they mothers for every damn thing ...

VENNIE. I'm sorry.

MAYDEE. *(Enters.)* I'm not hurt ...

VENNIE. I wasn't blaming you ...

MAYDEE. Really, I'm not hurt. If that's how you feel ...

LOLA. Look like every week on one of my programs they got some crazy that's killed somebody or raped somebody or can't keep a job or got some other kind of problem and who they say is the cause? They mother! *(Possessively puts her arm around MaDear.)* It's a damn shame that the woman responsible for bringing you into this world got to hear you rise up one day and blame her for every ill that comes your way ... bunch of ungrateful S-O-B's ... makes the hair on the back of my ass rise ...

MAYDEE. Mama please!

LOLA. Don't Mama me. It gets on my last nerve.

MAYDEE. All I was doing was trying to get her to think about her future ...

LOLA. The day you decided to use psychology on that child instead of a good ass whippin' was her day of ruin!

VENNIE. I'm sorry. Lord, let me get with the program and come correct. Let me shut my sorry behind up. I'm sorry. I'm very very sorry. How many more sorrys is it gon' take to get me in mother heaven again this evening?

RAISA. *(Laughs loudly, everyone turns around and looks at her.)* This is just like being home. I swear. This could be my mother's living room.

LOLA. Oh, your people have money too?

MAYDEE. Mama …

RAISA. No, I meant how sometimes my mother rakes me over the coals, she does the same thing, except she grabs her chest and has heart palpitations. *(Acting out her mother with heavy accent.)* You wanna kill me … why don't you just put a knife to my chest? Here, here's the bread knife, the same one I used to cut up your little sandwiches with. Here, take it and take my heart right along with it. For this I suffered, forty-two hours of labor, two days in a coma … a month in recovery … wait till you're a mother, may you know my pain … our life savings to send you to college for us to get back a refund, a pregnant drop-out, that's our refund. Miss Artist. Feh! *(Collapses laughing.)*

MAYDEE. *(Laughs and pats Raisa condescendingly, then in a show of unity, puts her arm around Lola's shoulder, to Raisa.)* Well, of course dear, we're a little different in this family. We've always supported Vennie and her dreams. I worked three jobs … sometimes it was four, wasn't it Mama?

LOLA. Oh, shoot, get outta here, sometimes I think you was working five jobs! You worked like a fool on fire!

MAYDEE. I wanted to make sure Vennie always had the best.

LOLA. And I took care of my little Pick-Me-Up when her mother was too busy working to be a real mother to her, ain't that right baby? Sometimes I had to be both mother and father …

MAYDEE. And I never, ever like the idea of using guilt to control my daughter …

LOLA. No, no. Chile, we ain't what you would call a guilt family …

VENNIE. *(Laughs.)* Y'all are real comedians. You two don't even listen to each other …

LOLA. I heard every word your mother said and I very much agree.

MAYDEE. I simply said …

VENNIE. That's why I don't think I want children. It does a job on your vision.

RAISA. I know it did a job on mine. I planned to be real open, everything my mother was, I planned to be the opposite. But the first time my son had an erection I panicked. I started screaming. *(Screaming.)* Stop that, stop that right now. Don't you touch your penis and testicles. Scared the poor lamb half to death, he 'bout fell back in the tub. Well, at least I used the proper words … penis and testicles ...

LOLA. *(Finally.)* Umph! How old you say your son was?

RAISA. Five.

LOLA. And his pee-pee getting hard? *(The phone rings, pandemonium.)*

VENNIE. I'll get it.

LOLA. *(Overlapping.)* No, I'll get it.

MAYDEE. *(Overlapping.)* No, I'll get it. I bet it's the call. I'll get it.

MADEAR. *(Overlapping, repeats.)* It's the man ... It's de man callin' for me ... It's de man ...

LOLA. *(Overlapping, pulling MayDee back.)* If that's Jimmy tell him ... tell him ... tell him I can meet him ...

MAYDEE. Would you let go of me? *(Picks up the phone.)* Hello. Oh, yes Dean Claudet ...

MADEAR. *(Wailing.)* I gots to git home.

LOLA. Mama, this is your home.

MADEAR. Dis ain't my home. *(Continues to cry loud and hit at them the more they try to console her.)* Dis ain't my home ...

LOLA. Stop that crying now. This is your home, Mama. Some people don't even have a place to lay their head, ain't gotta pot to piss in and here you are living nice, like a queen ... got your own room, your own TV and you still complaining, we could have you in a home somewhere ...

VENNIE. Don't tell her that. We would never put her in a home.

LOLA. We?!

RAISA. *(Overlapping.)* Should I get her some water?

LOLA. No. Don't pay her no mind. She does this all the time. Just trying to get some attention ... you know you's grown once and a child twice. She just workin' on her second childhood.

MADEAR. *(Overlapping, louder.)* Dis ain't my home. *(Screaming.)* Dis ain't my home. *(MaDear keeps screaming and wailing.)* Dis ain't my home. Man, dis ain't my home ... Dis ain't my home ...

LOLA. Mama, stop that screaming. Stop showing out now. *(Yelling in MayDee's direction.)* I told you she didn't need anything to drink.

VENNIE. *(Overlapping, stroking.)* MaDear, sssh, it's okay. It's okay ... Sssh, Mother's on the phone.

LOLA. *(Overlapping.)* Did you hear me Mama? Stop that screaming. Stop it right now. I'm a spank you ... I'll spank your little legs if you don't stop that noise ...

VENNIE. *(Overlapping.)* You hit her?

MAYDEE. *(Overlapping, hand over the phone.)* MADEAR, SHUT UP RIGHT NOW!

VENNIE. *(Yells at MayDee.)* DON'T TELL HER TO SHUT UP.

LOLA. Go 'head and take your call. *(Puts her hand over MaDear's mouth.)* I got it covered ... *(MayDee goes back to her call.)*

VENNIE. Why do you all treat her like this? You have her sitting around here like some museum piece ... She has feelings ... .

LOLA. Now you wait a minute, young lady. You bring your hippie-looking behind home every other year ... *(MaDear bites Lola's hand.)* Ouch! Shit. You bit me ... Mama, you bit me ...

MADEAR. Miss Raisin, come on. We gotta make a break for it ...

RAISA. Miss Dawkins, I ...

LOLA. *(Overlapping.)* Mama, you ain't going nowhere. And you bit me. I should take those teeth out your mouth right now. You can sit there and gum yourself silly for the rest of the day ... Father, deliver me. *(Dramatically raises her arms to the ceiling.)* Just give me a sign ... any sign ...

VENNIE. I oughtta take her back with me ...

LOLA. *(Up to the ceiling.)* That's close, but not quite. *(MayDee, overlapping, hangs up the phone, walks slowly toward MaDear, everybody freezes, no one can read her intentions. Using her body to shield MaDear.)* Now MayDee, Mama can't help herself ... she's the only Mama I got ... One door closes, baby, another one'll open ... I declare it will ...

VENNIE. *(Using her body to shield Lola.)* Mother, maybe next year.

MAYDEE. *(Crosses to MaDear, gives her a big kiss.)* You know I love you, old woman. Let's go plant some flowers right now. Everybody, I have arrived! *(Picks up the T-shirt, hugs it happily to her chest, starts dancing around, everyone hugs and is equally excited.)* I have arrived ...

LOLA. Oh baby, I'm so happy! I prayed on this. Mama is just so happy, I'm about to wet my pants. Thank you Jesus! Oh, I almost forgot.

VENNIE. I'm so happy for you, Mother. I knew you'd get it though.

LOLA. *(Overlapping.)* I put a surprise way back in your Frigidaire just for this occasion. I knew you was gonna get it. *(While Lola hunts in the back of the refrigerator for the bottle, MayDee crosses to the front door and opens it wide and yells.)*

MAYDEE. *(Yells.)* People, I have arrived.

LOLA. Shout, baby girl! Tell the world. My baby! Whew, I'm just getting so full. Shoot, I may have to lose a little water before it's over. *(To MayDee holding the bottle up.)* Look what Mama got you, baby. I ain't never spent this kind of money for something that wasn't a hundred proof.

MAYDEE. MayDee Lakeland has arrived! I have arrived!

VENNIE. Well yeah … Me too, Mother. Raisa and I are going to Europe. Just came home to say good-bye and maybe get the rest of my money … Okay? *(MayDee, Lola and MaDear stare at Vennie in disbelief as the lights go down.)*

Scene 2

At lights, we see Vennie and Raisa happily helping MaDear plant a garden under the tree. Inside the house, Lola studies herself in the mirror, adjusts her wig, and then applies lipstick. She stops for a minute to really take in her reflection. It's clear she doesn't like what she sees. She pulls her skin taut, then lets it go, sucks in her stomach, then sighs heavily. She then crosses to the phone, picks it up, listens then resignedly returns it to the cradle. She notices Vennie's boom box, turns it on to the sound of booming Motown music. At the sound of the music, Lola's spirit gradually returns …

LOLA. *(Dancing and singing with herself.)* Hey now … *(She crosses to the door and calls out.)* Somebody come in here and dance with me … *(Vennie enters and begins dancing with Lola. The two both dance with abandonment. Some moves are obvious moves Lola taught Vennie long ago and now Vennie has enhanced them with some new hip-hop moves. Lola attempts to follow but is not quite getting Vennie's*

60

moves, although she thinks she is. She is wearing her new T-shirt over her clothes. Raisa smiles as she watches them. Vennie beckons for her to join in, which Raisa eventually does. Raisa also tries to include MaDear in the dance by taking her arms and swinging them. MaDear watches child-like, obviously intrigued with the dancing.)

VENNIE. You have to use your arms more. *(Demonstrates.)* Like this.

LOLA. What you think I'm doing ... shit. S'cuse me, Raisa. *(She tries again.)*

RAISA and VENNIE. *(Chanting.)* You got it ... Go 'head ... Go Lola, go 'head ...

MAYDEE. *(Storms in from the hallway, holding her head, she looks around, spots them outside.)* It's too loud. Can you turn it down? *(No one hears her.)* I said can we ... *(Fuming, she clicks off the music.)*

LOLA. Hey.

MAYDEE. Didn't you hear me say it was too loud?

VENNIE. We didn't hear you.

MAYDEE. I guess not.

LOLA. Me and these girls were just having a little fun. I like this Raisa. She ain't no shortstop on this dancing.

RAISA. I used to not dance at all. Vennie taught me.

LOLA. Well you's a credit to your race now. Come on let's show MayDee. MayDee, put the music back on.

MAYDEE. I will not.

LOLA. Come on, just for a minute. *(Demonstrating.)* It's so cute ...

VENNIE. Forget it, MaLola. Everybody was having too much fun. A misdemeanor in this house ...

MAYDEE. *(Furious.)* That's it. *(Everybody sheepish as Lola puts on her act.)*

LOLA. Wasn't tryin' to be bad folk. Wasn't tryin' to be loud and upset all the neighbors your mama done lost all her hair worrying about. For the life of me, Lola just don't know how to be a good colored role model. But I tries. But no matter what I do, I'm a bad snapshot for my people, right MayDee? Thank God we got your Mama to elevate our race. Guess I'll get on back to this cake. Was on forty I think ... I don't know if all ninety of these candles gon' fit ... *(Starts counting candles for the cake.)*

MAYDEE. Raisa, if you'll excuse us.

RAISA. Sure. *(She exits.)*

LOLA. Maybe I was on thirty-nine ... *(Starts counting candles for the cake. Vennie starts to exit.)*

MAYDEE. Not so fast.

VENNIE. Almost made a clean break ...

LOLA. MayDee, I'm so glad about you getting that call. Who would've ever thought I'd raise a college professor ... Pick-Me-Up, baby, you wanna help MaLola count?

MAYDEE. I'm very upset.

LOLA. MayDee, maybe you should take one of your pills and have a little nap. We'll call you when we get everything ready ...

MAYDEE. Mama, did you hear me? I said I'm ...

LOLA. Shit, MayDee you always upset ... All we was doing was having a little fun. I'm so glad my baby's home. My Pick-Me Up ...

MAYDEE. She is not your Pick-Me-Up. She happens to be my daughter ... mine ... And I have not had one moment alone with her since ...

LOLA. Well, shit ... let me outta here. You only got to tell me once when I'm not wanted. I'll go sit with Raisa and the crazy one ... y'all call us when we allowed back in the front of the house. *(She exits. Silence for a moment.)*

VENNIE. So. I thought you said all you had to say earlier. You're not giving me the money. You don't care if I go across the street let alone to Europe. I can sink or swim because it's not your boat ... did I leave anything out...?

MAYDEE. Stop it.

VENNIE. Stop what?

MAYDEE. You're right. I don't like you.

VENNIE. And? What am I supposed to do, cry? Tell me something I don't already know ...

MAYDEE. You are selfish, arrogant and spoiled rotten ... And I don't like it. I don't like that I had anything to do with creating what you are at this moment. If I could do it over again I probably wouldn't have bothered ...

VENNIE. I wish you hadn't. Would've saved us both some trouble. I could've done nicely without being reminded every day how much a bother I was.

MAYDEE. I never made you feel like that.

VENNIE. Of course not. You were too busy keeping me preoccupied. Keep the child busy ... guaranteed to help you forget she exists ...

MAYDEE. Oh, so we're going to play my favorite game, poor deprived Vennie. It must be hard having such a meanie for a mother. A mother who tried to expose you to ...

VENNIE. Yeah, you exposed me all right. I had a great time being carted off or should I say dropped off ... Vennie and her activities ... You ever remember going to any of 'em with me? You ever want to hear about 'em when I got home? Even more basic, were you ever home?

MAYDEE. I had to work. You had to eat ...

VENNIE. Yeah, by myself. If it hadn't been for MaLola, I wouldn't had nothing ...

MAYDEE. *(Automatically corrects.)* Anything.

VENNIE. Sorry. Anything. This lecture over?

MAYDEE. I was home when I could be. And who made sure you had a home?

VENNIE. You, Mother.

MAYDEE. I didn't want to be gone all the time Vennie, but I didn't have a choice ...

VENNIE. Yeah right. Can I go now? *(Starts to exit but is stopped by the plea in MayDee's voice.)*

MAYDEE. All of this was for you ... You kept me working, kept me wanting to do more ... I wanted you to be proud of me ...

VENNIE. I am. I just don't know you.

MAYDEE. You can have the money.

VENNIE. I don't want it.

MAYDEE. I was just holding on to it ... maybe you would finish your education. I been saving that money since you were five Vennie ... I wasn't saving it for you to throw away ...

VENNIE. My career is throw away?

MAYDEE. I didn't say that. But going all the way to Europe on a chance is ... is ... stupid!

VENNIE. I said I didn't want the money ...

MAYDEE. *(On a roll.)* You know how many singers there are? Every black girl in the world wants to be a singer. Hundreds. How many will make it? Maybe one. Two at the most. And believe me sweetheart, you "ain't" that special to be one of 'em. No, I'm just not going to do it, Vennie. That money was for your future. I saved fifty thousand dollars for your damn future. I wore the same coat for six years, stockings with holes in 'em, didn't know what it was to own more than one pair of shoes ... got off one job and ran to the next ...

VENNIE. *(Overlapping.)* And ran to the next. As usual, you did it all ... I did have a father ...

MAYDEE. Father! You really do live in a dream world, don't you? Your father! Only thing he was ever good at was disappearing.

VENNIE. Disappearing!? You drove him away, like you drive everybody away.

MAYDEE. Yeah, so what's your excuse?

VENNIE. Hey, I'm trying to go. I'm trying to go around the world so you won't have to look at my face ever again.

MAYDEE. Look, I didn't mean what I said. I didn't have anything against your father. He got me out of the house ...

VENNIE. Yeah. Yeah. I've heard this before ...

MAYDEE. I never wanted you to make the same mistake ...

VENNIE. Oh you made sure of that. No little crumb-snatchers 'round here.

MAYDEE. Oh please. You didn't want a child Vennie, you just wanted to slap me in the face.

VENNIE. Yeah, that's all I was thinking about.

MAYDEE. *(Beat.)* I'm trying here, Vennie. I don't want to argue. I don't want to argue. I just ... You know I didn't want to be a mother, never did, but when I found out I was pregnant, I had this inkling that maybe you'd be a girl. And you know, surprisingly, that gave me joy. If I had to have a child, I prayed, please make it a daughter ... I knew ...

VENNIE. Knew what, Mother?

MAYDEE. I knew I'd love you ... I thought I'd finally have something special.

VENNIE. But then you got me ... a paper doll that didn't fit the cut-out.

MAYDEE. I knew firsthand how much a daughter could love her mother. Sure I made mistakes Vennie, but I kept working, hoping

64

that if I just worked hard enough ... one day you'd forgive me for whatever mistakes I made along the way and grab a hold to that future that I never had. A future I worked like a dog to give you. No, I didn't want you to be a mother at sixteen, saddled to some man ... struggling, hating yourself, hating me because I didn't protect you ... I wanted ...

VENNIE. I ... I ... I ... Always I. What you want. Always for you, isn't it?

MAYDEE. You damn straight. I'm your mother. I'm entitled. Why do you think any parent puts up with the shit you children dish out? Because we like it? No, it's because one day we're hoping that you'll wake up and stop treating us like jackasses, one day, one glorious day you'll prove to us that every sacrifice we made was worth it. If you don't want to do it for yourself, then yes dammit do it for me.

VENNIE. No, I wanna sing. I want my dream ... Just because you gave yours up doesn't mean I have to.

MAYDEE. I didn't give my dream up. It was taken from me.

VENNIE. Yeah, whatever. I can always finish school later ...

MAYDEE. Bullshit, Vennie! Six years and three schools later, you still haven't finished. You don't like the teachers ... you don't like the school ... you don't like their politics ... so you just up and quit. One semester left and you quit. Again! Just like you do every job, every apartment ... What do you have to show for my thirty five thousand two hundred and thirty something dollars? *(Lola has entered, unbeknownst to them.)* Nothing! No paper. No graduation. No skills. Nothing! Your damn dream! Well, if you're going to Europe, baby, you're going on a wing and a prayer because your behind's not getting another dime from me. You got some kind of gall even asking ... This was supposed to be my day and you wouldn't even let me have that. My entire family was supposed to be here to support me. Me! You do understand the meaning of the word, don't you? The one moment in my entire sorry life that I've been happy and you robbed me of even that. Just snatched it away with another one of your simple-ass whims to get my money. Well I'm not letting you rob me of another damn thing, Vennie. You hear that? Did you give one thought to me or your great-grand-mother who's turning ninety today ... bringing her a bag of damn dirt. Did you really think some cheap ass T-shirts and some half-dead weeds were enough to seal the deal…? And what was Raisa for, your poster child?

VENNIE. *(Deeply wounded.)* You just have to attack anything that's special to me, don't you?

MAYDEE. Special today, who knows about next week?

VENNIE. I don't know, Mother. She may not even be alive next week.

MAYDEE. Well, lucky for you. You won't have to sustain a commitment for long.

LOLA. MAYDEE!

VENNIE. I'm out of here … *(Vennie starts to walk away.)*

LOLA. *(To Vennie.)* Don't you move a step. You woman enough to dish it out, you better stand there and be woman enough to take it in. What I heard true? You lied to me, Vennie? You never graduated?

VENNIE. No.

LOLA. *(Very hurt.)* But your mama told me you did. She said you didn't walk, but she was going anyway to see if she could talk you in to it. She wouldn't let me go 'cause she knew I would've beat your trifling ass till you crawled across the stage.

VENNIE. MaLola, I …

LOLA. What the hell was you doing? That was some of my money in that fifty thousand. I sacrificed …

VENNIE. I tried to tell you …

LOLA. You didn't try that hard. MaLola didn't wanna see this day … I don't care if you wanna sing or sell pussy, but you was supposed to get that piece of paper first. I told everybody you graduated … that I had me two graduates … And you lied to me? You was this family's hope … and you lied to me, Vennie? Ain't nothing left for me now but Jesus …

VENNIE. *(Going to hug her.)* I'm sorry, MaLola. I didn't want to disappoint you. I'm sorry.

MAYDEE. You're sorry? You tell her, you sorry? What about me? Where's my sorry? Shit. I'm your mother.

VENNIE. MaLola, I'm planning to finish school …

MAYDEE. Most of that money was mine. She put in a thousand, maybe two, but the other forty-seven was mine, my sweat, my sacrifice. Mine! And you have the nerve to turn around and tell her, you sorry …

LOLA. *(Cradling Vennie.)* MayDee calm down … the child feels bad enough …

MAYDEE. No, Mama. Don't tell me to calm down. And you got your nerve sitting there like you so disappointed. *(sarcastically.)* Your sacrifice. Your two graduates. You may have made me but you didn't make this graduate. Where were you when I was trying to go to school? Huh? Where was your sacrifice then? Both of you make me sick.

LOLA. You wait just a minute, heifer. I helped you when I could … Damn near raised this child …

MAYDEE. Yeah, anything to make up for not raising your own. Too busy letting your men have fun with her. *(Lola slaps MayDee. MayDee raises her hand to slap her back.)*

LOLA. Go 'head. I dare you.

VENNIE. *(Getting in the middle of them.)* Stop. Stop. Please stop. Please. *(To MayDee.)* Oh, Mama … I didn't know … *(Reaches to hug MayDee who immediately turns and moves away.)*

LOLA. *(Crossing to the cake, dismissively.)* Wasn't nothing to know. *(Starts counting the candles. There is a moment of silence as each wrestles with the pain of it all.)*

VENNIE. *(More to herself than anyone in particular.)* I'm sorry … Maybe I shouldn't've come home … You're right. No matter what, I always seem to screw things up … I promise I really will finish school. *(No response so after a moment, frantically starts straightening the room.)* We're supposed to be having a party … we got the cake going on. What else do we need? How about a little music? You want another drink MaLola? Mama, I can fix you something. MaLola…? *(No response. Raisa wheels MaDear in. Raisa has decorated MaDear's hair with flowers.)* Hey now. Look at MaDear. Look at the birthday girl.

RAISA. Did we hear somebody mention a party? Doesn't the birthday girl look beautiful?

VENNIE. *(Grateful for the diversion.)* Yes. Yes. MaDear, you look so beautiful. *(Kisses her.)* I love you. We all love you. Don't we? *(No response.)* And we've had such good news today. Mother getting tenure. I told you all the way here that she was going to get it, didn't I Raisa? About how proud I was of her …

MAYDEE. *(Not looking at Lola, softly.)* How could you have not known, Mama?

VENNIE. I know I don't show it but I'm really proud of you, Mother. *(MayDee doesn't respond.)*

MAYDEE. You never could see past his smile, could you?

LOLA. Leave me be, MayDee. I gotta count these candles ... *(A little loud.)* Forty-one, forty-two ...

VENNIE. Mother, maybe we can ...

MAYDEE. Stay out of this Vennie ...

LOLA. Don't do this MayDee. I didn't know ...

MAYDEE. Because keeping that man was more important ... He was always more important.

MADEAR. *(Very agitated.)* My anniversary. Man was mine ...

LOLA. Don't start that Mama ... please ... Vennie, take her in the back. No, don't take her in the back, let's have the party ... right now ... Pick-Me-Up, put some music on ... Mama, come on ... where's those party hats I got you...?

MAYDEE. You knew, didn't you. Somewhere you had to have known what he was doing to me ...

LOLA. MayDee, don't do this. He was just being a father. You always needed more attention ... that's what he said ...

MAYDEE. And you believed him? Is that why you always sent him to pick me up from my lessons? Everybody thought that was so wonderful. How proud my stepfather was of me and my piano playing ...

LOLA. He was proud. Lord, Willie was so proud of you and your playing ... just like my daddy was proud of me and my dancing ...

MAYDEE. Yeah, so proud I had to keep playing for him all the way home in the backseat. I hated that car ... I hated my lessons and more importantly, I hated you. I wasn't being careless about my hand, Mama. I broke it on purpose.

LOLA. You just lie. You just a damn lie. You fell. That's what you told me. You fell. You just a damn lie.

MAYDEE. Am I? Is that what you had to tell yourself ... what you keep telling yourself?

LOLA. You done bent me over, MayDee don't knock me down, not in front of my baby.

MAYDEE. She's not your baby!

68

LOLA. *(To Vennie.)* I was workin' all the time Pick-Me-Up. I wanted your mama to have the best of everything ... everything ... clothes, piano, toys, lessons. I was working so hard ... I bought us a place where nobody could ever put us out ...

MAYDEE. I didn't need all that, Mama. All I needed was you to be there to hold me and tell me, "Mama's here baby, and I'll never let anything hurt you again." Why couldn't you do that?

LOLA. Dredging up the past, MayDee, is only giving it a fresh odor.

MAYDEE. Is that all you have to say? That shit stinks?

LOLA. What you want? You want me to cry, I'll cry. You want me to say I'm sorry. I'm sorry. You want me to erase the past, I can't. You want me to apologize for trying to give you life that I never had, well, hell'll freeze first 'fore I'll apologize for doing the best I could. Yes dammit, sometimes shit happens to you and it stinks. So wipe your ass and go on.

MAYDEE. God, you are one sorry excuse for a mother.

VENNIE. *(To MayDee.)* You don't mean that.

LOLA. I didn't know but I put him out. I put him out for you 'cause Lord knows I'd be with that man today if it hadn't been for you ... I don't know what he did and I don't wanna know ...

MADEAR. *(Overlapping.)* ... You knew, ridin' on his hip ...

LOLA. I knew he was driving a wedge between us and that's all I needed to know ...

MADEAR. On my husband's hip. He wasn't for you. He was for me. I married him, he wasn't yos ...

LOLA. OH SHUT UP MAMA!

MAYDEE. *(Overlapping.)* If you wouldn't holler at her ... *(Soothing.)* MaDear, everything's okay ... We didn't mean to upset you.

MADEAR. I sees you, split-tail ... you in dat shed out back wid my husband ...

LOLA. He was teaching me to dance, that's all, Mama. He was teaching me to laugh. You made it so we had to sneak. You wouldn't let me dance, you wouldn't let me laugh. You wouldn't let me do a damn thing except work and hide out somewhere. *(To MayDee.)* You think I was no count as a mother, well this chick here got me beat hands down. *(To MaDear.)* He wasn't just yours, he was my Daddy and he was a good man, he would've done anything for me

69

and goddammit, I loved him with every breath I took ... *(To MayDee.)* and that's all I was trying to give you, a daddy to love.

MADEAR. Split-tail, I sees you ...

LOLA. My name is not split-tail. It's not Sister. It's Lola. Lola, Mama! *(The phone rings. And rings again.)*

MAYDEE. Why don't you just answer it. *(Icy sarcasm.)* Go ahead. I'm sure it's what you been waiting on, what you're always waiting on. *(Lola glares at MayDee, then answers the phone.)*

LOLA. *(In the phone.)* Hello, who's this? Oh, A.H. *(Irritated.)* Where else she gon' be A.H., with you?! *(To MaDear.)* Mama, it's your beloved son.

MADEAR. *(Happy.)* He comin' for me? *(She takes the phone from Lola, then in the phone.)* You comin' for me? What time you comin'? But I been waitin' all day ...

LOLA. Mama, give me the phone.

MADEAR. *(Pitiful.)* Man, you love me? Today's our anniversary. That's right, seventy years. Did you 'member this time?

LOLA. So that's why you been out of sorts. Mama, Papa's dead. Give me the phone now ...

MADEAR. I been practicin' dancin'. *(Sadly looking up at Lola.)* He ain't comin' ... He say he ain't comin'.

LOLA. *(Touched by MaDear's sadness.)* I'll talk to him, Mama.

MADEAR. He ain't comin'.

LOLA. *(Gently takes the phone from MaDear, then yells in the receiver.)* You triflin' son of a bitch ...

MADEAR. *(Overlapping.)* Sister, tell him I'll be ready ... tell him I been lookin' for him.

LOLA. Why did you even call, A.H.? It's her ninetieth birthday, for Christ's sake. Oh, kiss my ass. *(She slams the phone down on the cradle.)*

MADEAR. *(Whimpering.)* Did you tell him I was gon' dance wid him? I practic'd. I was gon' surprise him. Did you tell him how I gits cold here?

LOLA. *(Taking in a deflated MaDear, slowly lets her anger go.)* Come on Mama, stop looking so sad. A.H., I mean the good doctor told me he's gon' come see you soon, real soon. Come on, let Sister clean you up, get your face washed and get you ready for your party ... *(Lola helps MaDear up who exits mumbling.)*

70

MADEAR. *(Mumbling as she exits.)* I waited all day … I ain't ugly. I can dance. *(Lola starts to exit behind her, but then stops short at the hallway. Without looking at MayDee …)*
LOLA. I'm sorry about what happened to you, MayDee, God knows I am. It shouldn't have never happened. But what you did about it and what you didn't do about your own damn dreams after that, well that ain't got nuttin' to do with me. I gave you life but it was up to you to make a life. I got my own regrets but I'll be damned if I'm about to carry yours too. So while you busy counting up all my sins, make sure you say a few prayers for yourself and for your child over there who you talked to today like she wasn't even yours. Now, I'm going to clean my Mama up and then I'm coming back in this room and we as a family are going to make sure she has a damn good party. *(On that Lola exits. MayDee watches them go, turning away from Vennie and Raisa. An awkward silence. Vennie looks at her mother, gets ready to approach, even reaches out a consoling hand.)*
VENNIE. Mother … *(No response from MayDee. Vennie is ready to give up, turns to Raisa, Raisa gestures for her to try again. But before Vennie can say anything, MayDee turns and addresses Raisa.)*
MAYDEE. *(With her usual formalness.)* Raisa, I'm truly sorry that you had to witness such antics … I apologize for my behavior and that of my family …
RAISA. Oh this was nothing. Visit my house sometimes, talk about walking a tightrope … every hour somebody's falling off. But somebody's always there to catch 'em, maybe not always the way you want, but at least they have their hands up. As Mother would say, love looks forward, hate looks back, but family has eyes all over its head.
VENNIE. What?
RAISA. Don't ask me. She talks in parables all the time, *(To MayDee.)* kind of like your mother.
MAYDEE. *(Smiles in spite of herself.)* Yes, she does talk, doesn't she?
VENNIE. Yeah, but she makes sure she's missed when she leaves a room. Now that's the kind of woman I wanna be when I grow up.
MAYDEE. Well, perhaps you're well on your way.
VENNIE. I hope that was a compliment. *(MayDee smiles at Vennie.)*

71

MAYDEE. You're more like her than I ever was. Raisa, do you love your mother?

RAISA. Yes.

MAYDEE. And how come?

RAISA. I guess because she's the longest relationship I've had in my life and that counts for a lot right about now.

MAYDEE. Well, you appear to be a very loving daughter. Your mother is a fortunate woman.

VENNIE. I never said I didn't love you ...

MAYDEE. *(A pause, as MayDee waits, hoping for Vennie to reassure her that she indeed does love her but nothing to that effect is forthcoming, finally.)* So you didn't. Well, why don't we just make your dream come true on your dime. I've decided to retire from motherhood. Maybe I'll take what used to be your "future" money and carve me out a little present. How does that sound?

VENNIE. Mother, this isn't for me, not totally ...

MAYDEE. Oh but it is. And as you have said to me on more than one occasion, it is your life, so every choice in it from here on out, sweetheart, needs to be yours, totally ...

VENNIE. I'm going. I'll find a way.

MAYDEE. No doubt. You're my daughter. If nothing else, you come from a long line of survivors so whatever you decide, you'll make it. *(Takes tableware out.)* Why don't you two make yourself useful. *(Vennie gets ready to object.)* Give me a break. Just do it ... Your mother is going to make herself a nice stiff drink, *(Which she does.)* put her feet up ... *(Which she does.)* and try to figure out how many ways a little money can say I love you. *(Toasting herself as she clicks on some music, her type of soothing music.)*

VENNIE. What did you say?

MAYDEE. Nothing. *(MayDee eases back, relaxed for the first time. It's short-lived though. The phone rings.)*

LOLA. I'll get it. I'll get it. *(Comes flying in the room.)* It's for me. I said I got it! *(MayDee smiles to herself — life is back to normal. In the phone.)* Hello ... Oh Jimmy ... No, I wasn't busy. I'm glad you finally called ... Yes ...

MADEAR. *(Overlapping, can be heard before she's seen.)* Man? Man, is dat you callin' for me? Man? I'm comin'. I'm comin'. *(Entering with Lola's boa draped on her shoulder and wearing Lola's hat and carrying Lola's purse. She has smeared lipstick across her face, and is tapping her cane on the floor as if she's looking for something.)* See, I'm ready ... Man you ain't dead. I been waitin' for you. I been waitin for you all day. You didn't leave me here all by myself ... Go on now an Jar de floor ... See, I'm dressed up and pretty now ... just like you like, just like Lola Bit. You gon' dance wid me Man? *(Attempts a step or two.)* See, I's dancin' now. I's really dancin'. All you had to do was ask me Man and see I learned how ... we can jar de floor now ... I ain't ugly no mo ... I'm pretty like Lola ... Come on now Man, jar de floor ... show me that you wid me ... *(Lola stops talking as she watches MaDear. Vennie begins to stomp her foot, softly at first and then louder. MayDee eventually joins in. Lola hangs up the phone, joins in and then Raisa.)* I know you's wid me. You didn't leave me here all by myself ... *(The stomping continues.)* I cain't half hear y'all chil'ren. Let me feel you ... Let Mama feel you. Yes Lord. Take me home, take me home ... *(The stomping builds as the heartbeat between the generations resounds loudly.)* Y'all chil'ren better jar de floor. Yes Lord, jar dat floor! *(Lights.)*

End of Play

PROPERTY LIST

Radio
Liquor bottles
Mirror (MADEAR)
Cereal, milk, slice of melon, knife (MAYDEE)
Funnel (MAYDEE)
Bags of food, party decorations (LOLA)
House shoes (MAYDEE)
Cigarettes, lighter (LOLA)
Ashtray (MAYDEE)
Purse (LOLA)
Air freshener spray (MAYDEE)
Piece of candy (MAYDEE)
TV remote (MADEAR)
Coffee cup (LOLA)
"Happy Birthday" sign (LOLA)
Money (LOLA)
Wheelchair with horn (LOLA)
Packages (LOLA)
Large mirror (LOLA)
Woman's suit on hanger (MAYDEE)
Beer, joint (VENNIE)
Perfume (RAISA)
Camera (RAISA)
Knapsack (RAISA)
Coffee table book (RAISA)
Bow (RAISA)
Mints (RAISA)
Suitcases, bags (RAISA, VENNIE)
Tray of burned rolls (MAYDEE)
Oversized T-shirts (RAISA)
Shawl (RAISA)
Chips and dip (LOLA, MAYDEE)
Drink (LOLA)
Wine, wineglass (MAYDEE)
Bag of dirt with plants (VENNIE)
Towel, hair oil, comb, brush (MAYDEE)

Drink (VENNIE)
Itinerary (MAYDEE)
Lipstick (LOLA)
Cake with candles (LOLA)
Tableware (MAYDEE)
Drink (MAYDEE)
Boa, hat, purse (MADEAR)

SOUND EFFECTS

Radio music
Phone ring
Piano playing
Doorbell ring
Motown music

NEW PLAYS

★ **THE CREDEAUX CANVAS by Keith Bunin.** A forged painting leads to tragedy among friends. "There is that moment between adolescence and middle age when being disaffected looks attractive. Witness the enduring appeal of Prince Hamlet, Jake Barnes and James Dean, on the stage, page and screen. Or, more immediately, take a look at the lithe young things in THE CREDEAUX CANVAS…" *–NY Times.* "THE CREDEAUX CANVAS is the third recent play about painters…it turned out to be the best of the lot, better even than most plays about non-painters." *–NY Magazine.* [2M, 2W] ISBN: 0-8222-1838-0

★ **THE DIARY OF ANNE FRANK by Frances Goodrich and Albert Hackett, newly adapted by Wendy Kesselman.** A transcendently powerful new adaptation in which Anne Frank emerges from history a living, lyrical, intensely gifted young girl. "Undeniably moving. It shatters the heart. The evening never lets us forget the inhuman darkness waiting to claim its incandescently human heroine." *–NY Times.* "A sensitive, stirring and thoroughly engaging new adaptation." *–NY Newsday.* "A powerful new version that moves the audience to gasps, then tears." *–A.P.* "One of the year's ten best." *– Time Magazine.* [5M, 5W, 3 extras] ISBN: 0-8222-1718-X

★ **THE BOOK OF LIZ by David Sedaris and Amy Sedaris.** Sister Elizabeth Donderstock makes the cheese balls that support her religious community, but feeling unappreciated among the Squeamish, she decides to try her luck in the outside world. "…[a] delightfully off-key, off-color hymn to clichés we all live by, whether we know it or not." *–NY Times.* "Good-natured, goofy and frequently hilarious…" *–NY Newsday.* "…[THE BOOK OF LIZ] may well be the world's first Amish picaresque…hilarious…" *–Village Voice.* [2M, 2W (doubling, flexible casting to 8M, 7W)] ISBN: 0-8222-1827-5

★ **JAR THE FLOOR by Cheryl L. West.** A quartet of black women spanning four generations makes up this hilarious and heartwarming dramatic comedy. "…a moving and hilarious account of a black family sparring in a Chicago suburb…" *–NY Magazine.* "…heart-to-heart confrontations and surprising revelations…first-rate…" *–NY Daily News.* "…unpretentious good feelings…bubble through West's loving and humorous play…" *–Star-Ledger.* "…one of the wisest plays I've seen in ages…[from] a master playwright." *–USA Today.* [5W] ISBN: 0-8222-1809-7

★ **THIEF RIVER by Lee Blessing.** Love between two men over decades is explored in this incisive portrait of coming to terms with who you are. "Mr. Blessing unspools the plot ingeniously, skipping back and forth in time as the details require…an absorbing evening." *–NY Times.* "…wistful and sweet-spirited…" *–Variety.* [6M] ISBN: 0-8222-1839-9

★ **THE BEGINNING OF AUGUST by Tom Donaghy.** When Jackie's wife abruptly and mysteriously leaves him and their infant daughter, a pungently comic reevaluation of suburban life ensues. "Donaghy holds a cracked mirror up to the contemporary American family, anatomizing its frailties and miscommunications in fractured language that can be both funny and poignant." *–The Philadelphia Inquirer.* "…[A] sharp, eccentric new comedy. Pungently funny…fresh and precise…" *–LA Times.* [3M, 2W] ISBN: 0-8222-1786-4

★ **OUTSTANDING MEN'S MONOLOGUES 2001–2002 and OUTSTANDING WOMEN'S MONOLOGUES 2001–2002 edited by Craig Pospisil.** Drawn exclusively from Dramatists Play Service publications, these collections for actors feature over fifty monologues each and include an enormous range of voices, subject matter and characters. MEN'S ISBN: 0-8222-1821-6 WOMEN'S ISBN: 0-8222-1822-4

DRAMATISTS PLAY SERVICE, INC.
440 Park Avenue South, New York, NY 10016 212-683-8960 Fax 212-213-1539
postmaster@dramatists.com www.dramatists.com

NEW PLAYS

★ **A LESSON BEFORE DYING by Romulus Linney, based on the novel by Ernest J. Gaines.** An innocent young man is condemned to death in backwoods Louisiana and must learn to die with dignity. "The story's wrenching power lies not in its outrage but in the almost inexplicable grace the characters must muster as their only resistance to being treated like lesser beings." –*The New Yorker.* "Irresistable momentum and a cathartic explosion...a powerful inevitability." –*NY Times.* [5M, 2W] ISBN: 0-8222-1785-6

★ **BOOM TOWN by Jeff Daniels.** A searing drama mixing small-town love, politics and the consequences of betrayal. "...a brutally honest, contemporary foray into classic themes, exploring what moves people to lie, cheat, love and dream. By BOOM TOWN's climactic end there are no secrets, only bare truth." –*Oakland Press.* "...some of the most electrifying writing Daniels has ever done..." –*Ann Arbor News.* [2M, 1W] ISBN: 0-8222-1760-0

★ **INCORRUPTIBLE by Michael Hollinger.** When a motley order of medieval monks learns their patron saint no longer works miracles, a larcenous, one-eyed minstrel shows them an outrageous new way to pay old debts. "A lightning-fast farce, rich in both verbal and physical humor." –*American Theatre.* "Everything fits snugly in this funny, endearing black comedy...an artful blend of the mock-formal and the anachronistically breezy...A piece of remarkably dexterous craftsmanship." –*Philadelphia Inquirer.* "A farcical romp, scintillating and irreverent." –*Philadelphia Weekly.* [5M, 3W] ISBN: 0-8222-1787-2

★ **CELLINI by John Patrick Shanley.** Chronicles the life of the original "Renaissance Man," Benvenuto Cellini, the sixteenth-century Italian sculptor and man-about-town. Adapted from the autobiography of Benvenuto Cellini, translated by J. Addington Symonds. "[Shanley] has created a convincing Cellini, not neglecting his dark side, and a trim, vigorous, fast-moving show." –*BackStage.* "Very entertaining...With brave purpose, the narrative undermines chronology before untangling it...touching and funny..." –*NY Times.* [7M, 2W (doubling)] ISBN: 0-8222-1808-9

★ **PRAYING FOR RAIN by Robert Vaughan.** Examines a burst of fatal violence and its aftermath in a suburban high school. "Thought provoking and compelling." –*Denver Post.* "Vaughan's powerful drama offers hope and possibilities." –*Theatre.com.* "[The play] doesn't put forth compact, tidy answers to the problem of youth violence. What it does offer is a compelling exploration of the forces that influence an individual's choices, and of the proverbial lifelines—be they familial, communal, religious or political—that tragically slacken when society gives in to apathy, fear and self-doubt..." –*Westword.* "...a symphony of anger..." –*Gazette Telegraph.* [4M, 3W] ISBN: 0-8222-1807-0

★ **GOD'S MAN IN TEXAS by David Rambo.** When a young pastor takes over one of the most prestigious Baptist churches from a rip-roaring old preacher-entrepreneur, all hell breaks loose. "...the pick of the litter of all the works at the Humana Festival..." –*Providence Journal.* "...a wealth of both drama and comedy in the struggle for power..." –*LA Times.* "...the first act is so funny...deepens in the second act into a sobering portrait of fear, hope and self-delusion..." –*Columbus Dispatch.* [3M] ISBN: 0-8222-1801-1

★ **JESUS HOPPED THE 'A' TRAIN by Stephen Adly Guirgis.** A probing, intense portrait of lives behind bars at Rikers Island. "...fire-breathing...whenever it appears that JESUS is settling into familiar territory, it slides right beneath expectations into another, fresher direction. It has the courage of its intellectual restlessness...[JESUS HOPPED THE 'A' TRAIN] has been written in flame." –*NY Times.* [4M, 1W] ISBN: 0-8222-1799-6

DRAMATISTS PLAY SERVICE, INC.
440 Park Avenue South, New York, NY 10016 212-683-8960 Fax 212-213-1539
postmaster@dramatists.com www.dramatists.com

NEW PLAYS

★ **THE CIDER HOUSE RULES, PARTS 1 & 2 by Peter Parnell, adapted from the novel by John Irving.** Spanning eight decades of American life, this adaptation from the Irving novel tells the story of Dr. Wilbur Larch, founder of the St. Cloud's, Maine orphanage and hospital, and of the complex father-son relationship he develops with the young orphan Homer Wells. "...luxurious digressions, confident pacing...an enterprise of scope and vigor..." –NY Times. "...The fact that I can't wait to see Part 2 only begins to suggest just how good it is..." –NY Daily News. "...engrossing...an odyssey that has only one major shortcoming: It comes to an end." –Seattle Times. "...outstanding...captures the humor, the humility...of Irving's 588-page novel..." –Seattle Post-Intelligencer. [9M, 10W, doubling, flexible casting] PART 1 ISBN: 0-8222-1725-2 PART 2 ISBN: 0-8222-1726-0

★ **TEN UNKNOWNS by Jon Robin Baitz.** An iconoclastic American painter in his seventies has his life turned upside down by an art dealer and his ex-boyfriend. "...breadth and complexity...a sweet and delicate harmony rises from the four cast members...Mr. Baitz is without peer among his contemporaries in creating dialogue that spontaneously conveys a character's social context and moral limitations..." –NY Times. "...darkly funny, brilliantly desperate comedy...TEN UNKNOWNS vibrates with vital voices." –NY Post. [3M, 1W] ISBN: 0-8222-1826-7

★ **BOOK OF DAYS by Lanford Wilson.** A small-town actress playing St. Joan struggles to expose a murder. "...[Wilson's] best work since Fifth of July...An intriguing, prismatic and thoroughly engrossing depiction of contemporary small-town life with a murder mystery at its core...a splendid evening of theater..." –Variety. "...fascinating...a densely populated, unpredictable little world." –St. Louis Post-Dispatch. [6M, 5W] ISBN: 0-8222-1767-8

★ **THE SYRINGA TREE by Pamela Gien.** Winner of the 2001 Obie Award. A breathtakingly beautiful tale of growing up white in apartheid South Africa. "Instantly engaging, exotic, complex, deeply shocking...a thoroughly persuasive transport to a time and a place...stun[s] with the power of a gut punch..." –NY Times. "Astonishing...affecting ...[with] a dramatic and heartbreaking conclusion...A deceptive sweet simplicity haunts THE SYRINGA TREE..." –A.P. [1W (or flexible cast)] ISBN: 0-8222-1792-9

★ **COYOTE ON A FENCE by Bruce Graham.** An emotionally riveting look at capital punishment. "The language is as precise as it is profane, provoking both troubling thought and the occasional cheerful laugh...will change you a little before it lets go of you." –Cincinnati CityBeat. "...excellent theater in every way..." –Philadelphia City Paper. [3M, 1W] ISBN: 0-8222-1738-4

★ **THE PLAY ABOUT THE BABY by Edward Albee.** Concerns a young couple who have just had a baby and the strange turn of events that transpire when they are visited by an older man and woman. "An invaluable self-portrait of sorts from one of the few genuinely great living American dramatists...rockets into that special corner of theater heaven where words shoot off like fireworks into dazzling patterns and hues." –NY Times. "An exhilarating, wicked...emotional terrorism." –NY Newsday. [2M, 2W] ISBN: 0-8222-1814-3

★ **FORCE CONTINUUM by Kia Corthron.** Tensions among black and white police officers and the neighborhoods they serve form the backdrop of this discomfiting look at life in the inner city. "The creator of this intense...new play is a singular voice among American playwrights...exceptionally eloquent..." –NY Times. "...a rich subject and a wise attitude." –NY Post. [6M, 2W, 1 boy] ISBN: 0-8222-1817-8

DRAMATISTS PLAY SERVICE, INC.
440 Park Avenue South, New York, NY 10016 212-683-8960 Fax 212-213-1539
postmaster@dramatists.com www.dramatists.com